ATOM BOMB AND MISSILES IN ANCIENT INDIA

ATOM BOMB AND MISSILES IN ANCIENT INDIA

and Ancient War Weapons

S. NARAIN

KALPAZ

ISBN: 978-93-5128-250-1

Price: ₹ 540

First Published, 2017

Published by

Kalpaz Publications
C-30, Satyawati Nagar,
Delhi – 110052
E-mail: kalpaz@hotmail.com
Ph.: 9212142040

Printed at: G. Print Process, Delhi

Cataloging in Publication Data—DK
Courtesy: D.K. Agencies (P) Ltd. <docinfo@dkagencies.com>

Narain, S., author.
Atom bomb and missiles in ancient India : and ancient war weapons / S. Narain.
pages cm
Includes bibliographical references.
ISBN 9789351282501

1. Atomic bomb—India—History. 2. Weapons, Ancient—India. 3. Guided missiles—India—History. 4. India—History, Military. 5. Scientists—India—History. I. Title.

U821.I4N37 2016 DDC 355.820954 23

Tel. : 011-27871018
Fax : 91-11-2787102

दिल्ली इन्जीनियरिंग कॉलेज
(राष्ट्रीय राजधानी क्षेत्र दिल्ली सरकार)

सत्यमेव जयते

DELHI COLLEGE OF ENGINEERING
(Govt. of National Capital Territory of Delhi)

Prof. P.B. SHARMA
Ph.d. (B'ham, U.K.)
FIE, FAeroS, FWAPS

बवाना रोड, दिल्ली - 110 042
Bawana Road, Delhi - 110 042

E-mail : pbsharma@dce.edu

FOREWARD

The heritage of Science and Technology of India if sincerely and honestly deciphered, shall not only help us to understand and appreciate the magnificant heights of scientific and technological advancement in ancient India but shall also provide the much needed impetus to take the modern age of Information Technology driven developments to the unprecedented levels of wisdom propelled systems of tomorrow.

A sincere and systematic attempt in this direction has been made by Shri S. Narain in his treatise on "Atom Bomb and Missile in Ancient India. I am indeed happy to note that in the present work Shri Narain has elucidated the novel cause of scientific advancement in ancient India pursued by ancient India's scientists and technologists, wherein the scientists and engineers both worked relentessly for the development of a human society with scientific temper and technological acumen.

PROF. P.B. SHARMA
Principal & Dean (Faculty of Technology)
Delhi College of Engineering,
University of Delhi
also
Founder Vice-Chancellor
Rajiv Gandhi Technological University, Bhopal

PREFACE

The title of the book "ATOM BOMB AND MISSILES IN ANCIENT INDIA" may sound unbelievable to many a readers as these weapons are considered to be the products of modern science and technology. However, it is a fact that there has been a definite conception of *atom* forming the bedrock of modern atom bomb. There is a close similarity between the modern theory of atoms and that expounded by the ancients. Similarly there is mention of missiles in epic. Though the technology was primal one.

The book delves upon the kinds of missiles mentioned in ancient scriptures as well as treatment of atom in ancient India, and the reason of not developing atom bomb there upon. The kind of weapons used in various wars in ancient India right from Vedic period together with vehicles and organizations of army with various divisions may be an interesting reading. The life sketch and achievements of the eminent scientists of ancient India, who deserve full credit for taking the *Bharat Varsha* to a height of glory enviable to western countries have also been delineated.

S. NARAIN

CONTENTS

1

India
An Ancient Version

1

INDIA - AN ANCIENT VERSION

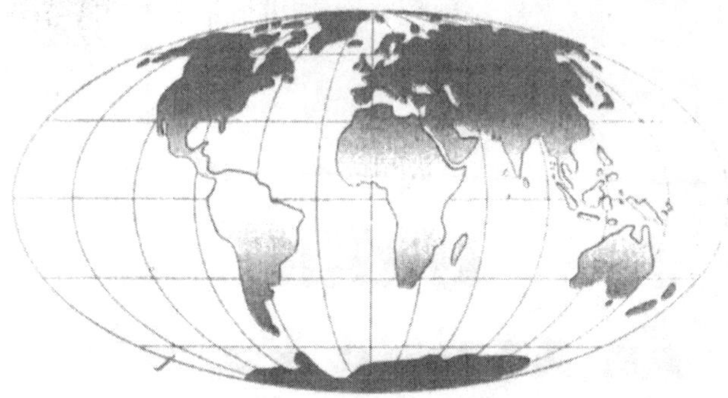

The sub contents of India stretching from Himalaya to the sea and from Kanyakumari to Kashmir fascinating the foreign countries with the tales of riches, prosperity and progress, according to ancient version is a part of a continent named as *Jambuduipa*[1] and the Earth as a whole has been conceived to have been divided into seven concentric island continents the inner most named as Jambuduipa. Infact it was not a fancy but was a territorial designation actually in use from 3rd Century B.C. and has been confirmed by the early Buddhist evidences. It is interesting to know that the Earth is conceived to have Been divided by modern geographers as well as by ancient consmographers, into seven continents.

Seven Continents According to Modern Geographers

1	2	3	4	5	6	7
Asia	Europe	Africa	South America	North America	Australia	Antarctica

Seven Continents According to Ancient Cosmographers

1	2	3	4	5	6	7
jamboo	Plaksha	Shalmalee	Kusha	Krauncha	Shaka	Push Kara

INDIA - BHARATVARSHA-AJNABHA

The physical and geographical entity known as India was earlier called as Bharat Varsha after the fam-ous and mighty, Bharata King as per Bhagwatpurana[2] (Chakravorty Samrata) who ruled a good part of this country for number of years and endeared himself to the masses for his bravery, righteouness and justice. He is believed to be the first ruler to initiate democracy in those foregone times. As the tale of his bravery goes, Bharata when he was a child of 5 or 6, would play with fierce wild animals like lions, tiger, leopard etc.opening their mouths and count their teeth even. The earliest name of the country was *Ajnabha* as per Bhagwadpurnaa a holy Hindu scripture. The term 'India' was applied by Greeks for the first time who came in this country in 326-327 BC on invasion of Alexander. The term Hindustan has been mentioned by medieval Historians (which is closely connected with Hindu) and is derived from Sindhu - the great river, which is a dominant feature of that part of the sub-continent where the Aryan Civilization flourished.

DIVISIONS AND STATES OF ANCIENT INDIA

In ancient literature we have reference to a five fold division of India as under :-

1) **Madhyadesha** - Central part of the Indo-Gangetic-plain stretching from the river Sarasvati, which flowed past Thanesa and Pehoa (ancient Prithudaka) to Allahabad and Benares.

2) **Brahmarshi-desa** - The western part of this area was known as the Brahmiarshi-desam.

3) **Uttarapatha or Udichya** - To the South of the Madhayadesa, beyond Pehoa, lay Uttarapatha or Udichya (North West India) to its west Aparanta or Pratichya (Western India).

4) **Dakshinapatha** - The Southern part was called Dakshinapatha or the Deccan.

5) **Purvadesa** - The eastern part was called Purvadesa or Prachya.

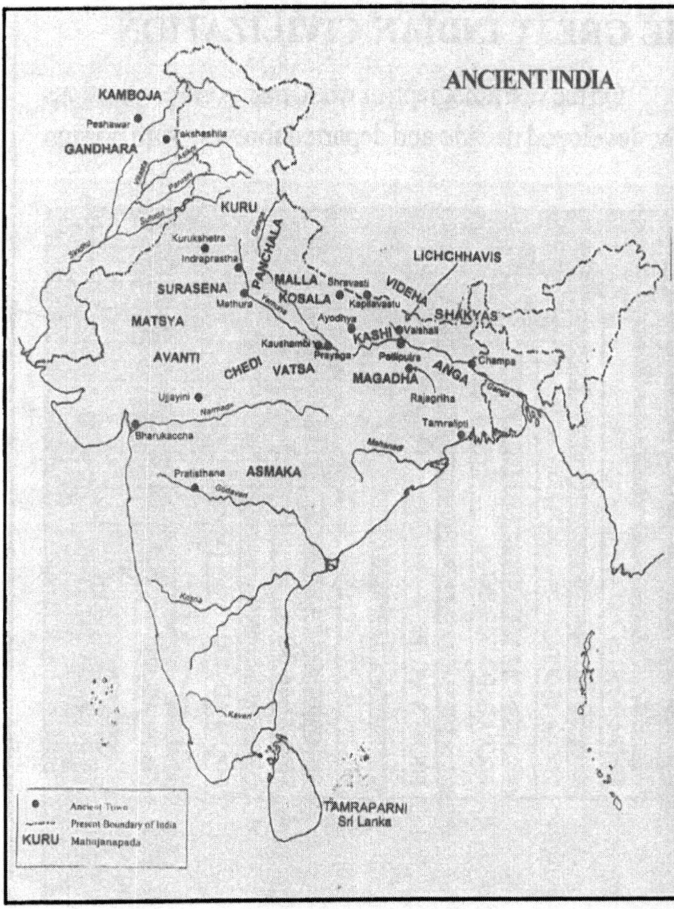

ANCIENT INDIA MAHAJANPADAS

The term Uttarapatha was at times applied to the whole of Northern India, and Dakshinapatha was in some ancient works restricted to the Upper Deccan North of the Krishna river the far South being termed Tamilakam or the Tamil country.

THE GREAT INDIAN CIVILIZATION

On the vast lithograph of world many on a civilizations grew, developed decade and departed forever, with no sign

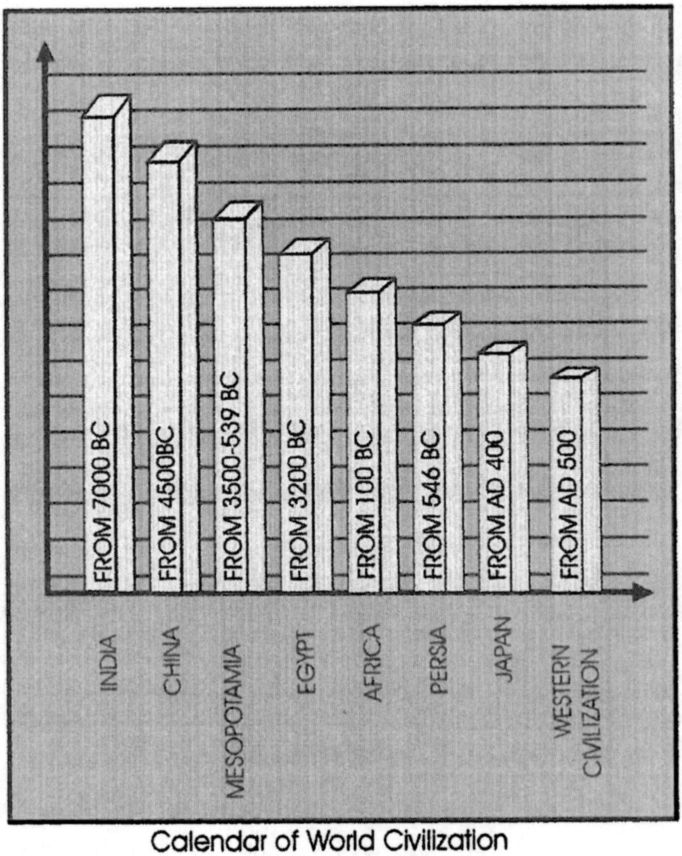

Calendar of World Civilization

of comeback leaving behind thin relics of them. However the Indian civilization which is perhaps the oldest living culture still surviving, through sometimes succumbed to the assault &

invasions of allien races but resurrected itself soon. Originating somewhere 7000 BC. It was a fairly developed civilization around 2500 BC as revealed by archaeological excavation in Indus valley region.

The Vedic period is, however, regarded as the real dawn of the present civilization called Aryan civilization belonging to the period of 1500-2000 BC, Believed to be the revealed words of God, Vedas are considered as the fountain head of spritual knowledge and even sciences. The Vedic mantras like 'Gayitri' hymn of Rig Veda is still chanted by hindus at every holy occasion. Yajnas are still performed with fire sacrifices with ghee, grains and other such materials on the occasion of birth, marriage and puja ceremonies. The Aryan civilization is still livid, and vibrant and going strong, speaking of its greatness.

Kumbh Mela - Congregation at Haridwar going on from ancient period

FOOTNOTES

1. अतः परं प्लक्षादीनां प्रमाणलक्षणसंस्थानतो वर्षविभाग उपवर्ण्यते।1। जम्बूद्वीपोऽयं यावत्प्रमाणविस्तारस्तावता क्षारोदधिना परिवेष्टितो यथा मेरुर्जम्ब्वाख्येन लवणोदधिरपि ततो द्विगुणविशालेन प्लक्षाख्येन परिक्षिप्तो यथा परिखा बाह्योपवनेन। प्लक्षो जम्बूप्रमाणो द्वीपाख्याकरो हिरण्मय उत्थितो यत्राग्निरुपास्ते सप्तजिह्वस्तस्याधिपतिः प्रियव्रतात्मज इध्मजिह्वः स्वं द्वीपं सप्तवर्षाणि विभज्य सप्तवर्षनामभ्य आत्मजेभ्य आकलय्य स्वयमात्मयोगेनोपरराम।2।

   Shrimad Bhagwat Purana 5.1-2

2. भरतस्तु महाभागवतो यदा भगवतावनितलपरिपालनाय सञ्चिन्तितस्तदनुशासनपरः पञ्चजनीं विश्वरूपदुहितरमुपयेमे।1। तस्यामु ह वा आत्मजान् कार्त्स्न्येनानुरूपानात्मनः पञ्च चनयामास भूतादिरिव भूतसूक्ष्माणि।2। सुमतिं राष्ट्रभृतं सुदर्शनमावरणं धूम्रकेतुमिति। अजनाभं नामैतद्वर्षं भारतमिति यत आरभ्य व्यपदिशन्ति।3।

   Shrimad Bhagwat Purana 7.2-3

3. Advanced History of India - R.C. Majumdar etc.

2

Ancient India : A Haven of Sciences

2

ANCIENT INDIA : A HAVEN OF SCIENCES

Ancient India was not only the land of spiritual knowledge but also a haven of positive sciences. It was not the land of beggars and snake charmers as ridiculed with the slandrous remarks by some foreigners but is a country striving for progress and advance ment in every sphere. The first writing script system was developed here and the Indus Valley civilization is regarded as the first urban civilization of Earth. Here the numeral zero was discovered, the fundamental input of all abstract sciences, the arithmetic, the beejganit, the geometry, the art and science of three angular characteristics, the Trigno metry and the entire horizon of mathematical domain of the cosmos was very well comprehended by our ancestors well before, the most of the other countries could grasp the enormous power of mathematics. It is surprising to know that the foundation of the laws of the thermodynamics were laid here, the bio-chemistry and the quantum physics were well understood & this provided our ancestors a conviction in the eternal existence of man both in its matter and the energy.

ANCIENT SCIENCES IN FOREIGN LANDS

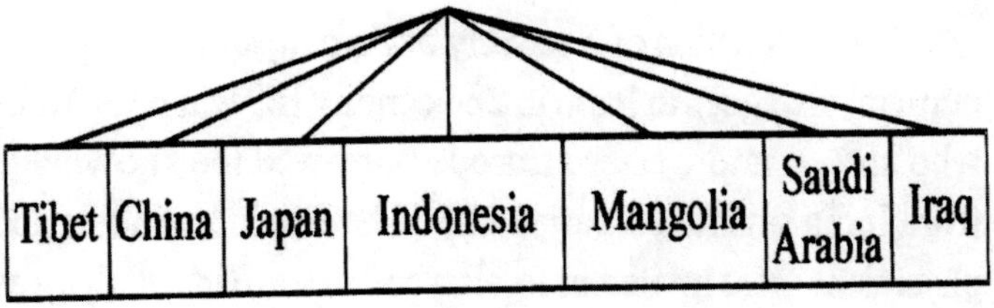

Yes, it is a fact that Indian thoughts and Indian sciences reached several countries like Indo-China, China, Japan, Mongolia, Indonesia etc. particularly in Asia. Ancient sciences had great influence even in later times and several Chinese travellers one after the another visited this country and studied in Indian university and returned their home country with new ideas. In Arabian countries, the Sanskrit literature was translated in Arabic or Persian to be read by the scholars of those countries to get new knowledge. The works of Brahma Gupta, the famous mathematician and astronomer of Ancient India were taken to Baghdad during AD 753-744 and were translated into Arabic to get new knowledge in mathematics and astronomy. The place value system was for the first time used by India which was later on adopted by Arabs who spread it in western world. The Indian numerals appeared in the western world.

The decimal system on which the mathematics is based, was used in India for the first time. The famous mathematician Arya Bhatta (AD 476-500) was acquainted with it. The Chinese, the Arabs all borrowed directly or indirectly from India.

The distinction of discovery of Zero treating it a separate numeral also goes to India in 2nd century BC where as Arabs who spread it to western Europe borrowed the knowledge from India several centuries after. The Hindu scientists and physicians were invited in foreign countries to install them as chief physicians of their hospitals and the famous books on various sciences i.e. pharmacology, toxicology on snakes veterinary and veterinary sciences etc. were got translated from Sanskrit to Arabic etc.

TECHNOLOGY AND CRAFTS IN ANCIENT INDIA

"At this time when the West Europe, the birthplace of modern industrial system, was inherited by uncivilized tribes, India was famous for the wealth of her rulers and for the high artistic skill of her craftsmen".

- Industrial Commision of India

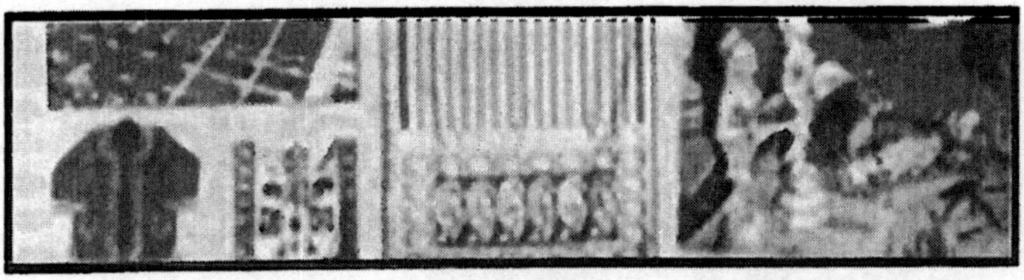

Textile Designs   Textile Technique   Lost Wax Casting

No doubt, ancient India was booming with a number of crafts and technology. The fine muslin of Dacca, the sculptures of post Buddhist era and the wonderful Ashoka Pillars, the number of which is between thirteen to fourteen, are the living testimonies to the fact that the ancient India was equally rich in skill and technology. The pillar at Delhi made of wrought iron in the time of Samundragupta, is a marvel of metallurgical skill. Mr.V.A.Smith a noted historian in his work 'Fine Art' observes with regard to the monolithic shaft of Ashoka column as under:

"The fabrication, conveyance and erection of monoiths of such enormous size-the heaviest weighting about 50 tonnes-are proofs that the engineers and stone cutters of Ashoka's age were not inferior in skill and resource to those of any time of country."

In fact the metallurgical skills of India are well manifest in the treatment of iron in the famous iron pillar at Delhi during the period. The surgery also made good strides as the advanced surgical processes including and performing a puncture has been mentioned by I.T. Sang.

PLETHORA OF CRAFTS & TECHNOLOGY

In many a Buddhist and Jain works there is mention of various technical arts and crafts which were called as 'kalas' and the traditional number has been mentioned as sixty four though some works mention more than 64 kalas. The details of traditional 64 kalas have been given in many works such as Kadambini, Kamsutra by Vatsayana etc. The disciplines of craft are Covered by the following technologies:

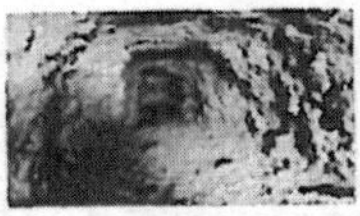

1. Metallurgy
2. Mine technology
3. Cooking technology

4. Leather technology
5. Textile design technology
6. Textile technology
7. Pottery technology

8. Machine fabrication technology
9. Dairy technology
10. Ship building technology

11. Gold technology
12. Weapon manufacturing technology

Archeological findings have confirmed that the following technologies were booming in Ancient India:

1. Zinc smelting

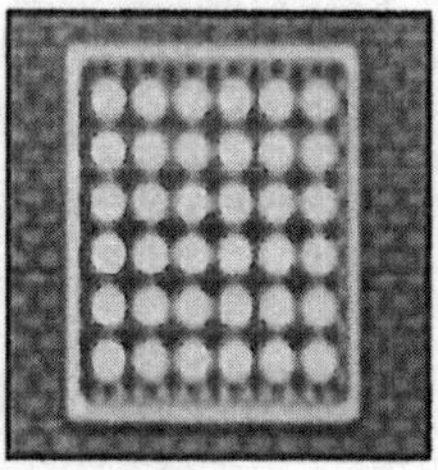

India is perhaps the first country to had technology for semi-industrial production of metallic zinc at the Jawararea of Rajasthan though zinc is the most difficult to smelt. However, using certain advanced technique by specifically designed retorts smelting was done.

2. Wootz steel

India was producing high quality steel before Christian era by using the crucible steel and in Gupta period it was exported to foreign countries for manufacturing quality swords.

3. Coin Technology

Casting Coin industry flourishing in ancient India and punch marked coins were in use in 6th century B.C. The coins were made of silver, copper, gold and different alloys like bronze which speaks that the technology was at advance state.

In fact each dynasty in ancient India made its coins different from the other one.

4. Lost Wax casting

This technology in India dates back to about 2500 B.C. at Indus Valley where in famous dancing girl statue was found. The lost wax method is well known technique for metal casting. Even in Gupta period a text Vishnu Samhita refers directly to the modeling of wax for making metal Objects.

5. Iron casting technology

India can raise its head with pride for the production of marvelous edifices like the iron pillar at Delhi which is still free from corrosion or rust even after thousands of years, using iron casting technology which speks that the ancients had mastered the technique.

6. Cotton Gin

Some scenes of Ajanta cave speak the use of cotton Gin technology in India as early as 5th-6th century A.D. the industrial revolution of Europe in 1793 improved this technology for the cotton Gin.

7. The science of Chemistry

The ancient name being 'Rasashala', this science saw a great progress in ancient India. As the archeological excavations at Takshila has evinced alcohol distillation. Nagarjuna was masterpiece in the field of Indian Alchemy-Rasashala and a laboratory depicting the use of number of types of Yantras forchemical purposes like distillation has been found suggesting the advancement of the science.

8. Glass work Technology

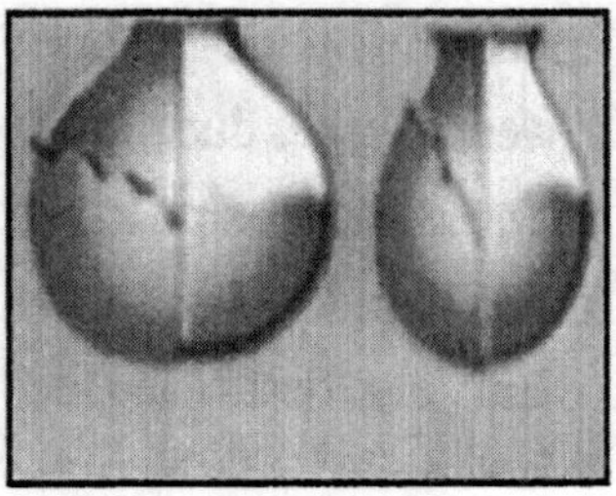

This technology was definitely in existence and elegant glass heads were found in Ganga valley dating back to 1000 B.C. Several glass objects of different colours have been found in many sites revealing the presence of the glass tech-nology in India.

This all speaks volume about the proficiency attained by us in art, science and technology which can only be conjectured by the works which have left behind and the skill and refinement with which they are designed and constructed. The most marvelous monuments of the age, the dexterity as well as the delicacy displayed in the manufacture of woolen, silken and cotton fabrics, the height of workmanship shown in the technical treatment of wood, metal and stone; the astounding technique of dress and ornaments; and the constructive enact ness manifested in preparing the products of peace as well as the weapon of war-give one a fat idea of the kind of technology and the quality of technical training and vocational knowledge imparted in those days.

DECADE AND DECLINATION

With the spate of foreign invasions, Takshila the oldest centre of learning of Hindu sciences and technical arts, with as many as over 50 institutions, having lost its character akin to an university, Nalanda - the famous university attracting students far and wide and one time having ten thousands of pupi,l went to ashes due to an avalanche, the further progress of ancient sciences came to a stop. The foreign invaders like Mehmood plundered and looted the prosperity and riches of this country also destroying the works of ancient sciences and technology, dealt deadly blow to our intellectual heritage making several sciences to vanish completely.

Nalanda University

FINAL COUNTDOWN

With the death of Harsha, a chapter of Indian History comes to a close. The steps of progress halted and decay set in. The rigidity of caste grew and the standard of professionalism suffered a definite setback as the technical skills become rigidly confined to the techniques and processes of their own vocation once evolved with no advancement. Gone were the glorious days of excellence of engineering skill behind the Ashoka Pillars, the town planning and the architecture of the palaces of the Emperor Harsha, the sculpture of post Buddhist period and so on. The progress made in medical surgery evolved in ancient period which earned high compliments even from Europeans, started decaying as not only dissection of human body but even a touch of dead body was considered enough to bring contamination. Even the handling of a lancet was discouraged, with the result that anatomy and surgery fell into disuse and become a dead science.

The 500 years of absolute peace resulted into degeneration of Hindus who become complacent "insular in ideas, without any knowledge of what was happening in the rest of the world", writes a noted historian, ***"Civilisation became decadent inbreed for lack of fertilising contacts with dissimilar cultures, society became static and the systematisation of previous ages like Chaturvema came to be accepted a divine regulations".*** **Alberuni -a famous Arab scholar who visited India in llth century A.D. draws a sad picture of bigotry of Hindus.**

"The Hindus believe that there is no country but theirs : no nation like theirs, no kings like theirs, no religion like theirs, no sciences like theirs. They are by nature niggardly to communicating that which they know, and they take the greatest possible care to withhold it from men of another caste, among their own, people, still much more, of course, from any foreigner. Accordingly to their belief, there is no other country on earth but theirs, no other race of man but theirs and no created beings besides them have any knowledge of science whatsoever .If you tell them of any science or scholar in Khurasan and Persia, they will think you to be both an ignoramus and a liar. If they travelled and mixed with other nations they would soon change their mind, for their ancestors were not as narrowminded as the present generation is."

One may not agree with the observation of Alberuni entirelyhow ever it is a fact that no advance in seen after that date in the realnus of sculpture Metallurgy, Surgery etc. with old learning getting stereotyped and started degenerating.

BIBLOGRAPHY

1. Alleruni's India (1031 A.D.)
2. Datta B.B. (1932)
   The science of sullas, Uni. of Calcutta.
3. Majumdar R.C. (1952 to 1965)
   The History and culture of Indian people.
4. A publication of National science centre, Delhi - OUR SCIENCE AND TECHNOLOGY HERITAGE.

3

Kanada

A Great Atomic Scientist Philosopher

3

KANADA : A GREAT ATOMIC SCIENTIST-PHILOSOPHER

In today's world atom bomb, nuclear bomb, hydrogen bomb and other new kind of nuclear devices are well-known and are considered to be the product of modern science. The first explosion of atom bomb by US took the world by surprise and made devastation to such a horrible extent that the cities of Hiroshima & Nagasaki of Japan became the graveyard of thousands & millions of people. The world was amazed to see the tremendous and uprecedented power of atom bombs.

It will however, be unbelievable that the concept of atom and the atomic theory in ancient way is the product of our great ancient scientists which was treated a philosophy but was true in regard to the concept of atom, Kanada is the first such great atomic scientist of ancient India. It is interesting to mention that there was no demarcation in ancient India between what we now call religion, philosophy & science and all these disciplines were utilized to explore the fundamental truth. This amalgamation of different aspects of knowledge led many foreign scholars to attach no significance to the scientific theories contained in them. It is only after we have rid ourselves of this bias, come to the conclusion that the scientific theories therein, though not based upon regular experiments in the laboratory but are worthy of consideration. This also holds good in case of Kanada.

The age of Kanada is believed somewhere around 600 B.C., however, his works were appreciated only in the 20th century and professor A.B. Keith in his book on Indian logic and Atomism published in 1921 gave an excellent account of some of the main thoughts developed in regard to the concept of matter and Atomic theory of Kanada. Though, in the Sacred books of Hindu's series an English translation of the Sutras of Kanada and commentary of Sankara Misra was published in the year 1911.

BIRTH AND AGE OF KANADA

The expounder of atomic theory is known by various names such as Aulukya, Kasyap and the more popular one - Kanada, whose treatise named as Vaisesika consists of 10 books, each of 2 chapters. From the various names by which Kanada is known, it transpires that he was the son of Uluka, a highly spiritual family of Kasyapa. As per "Modern Reveal" 1909, he belonged to Prabhasa[1] in Allahabad district and his teacher was Som Sarma and as per Puranas, he was regarded as incarnation of Lord Siva. Kanada lived the life of an ascetic and used for his daily bread, particle of rice scattered on public streets. As he would feed on particles, i.e. Kanas, he was known as Kanada, Kanabhaksa or Kanabhuk.[2]

As the story goes, Kanada pleased Lord Shiva the grand master of learning who delivered learning the truth contended in it, appointed him to compose a compendium.

THE VAISISIKA SUTRA

Kanada's sutras of Vaisesika system find reference in many ancient works like Vayu purana, Padam purana, Devi Bhagwati, Maha Bharta and other scriptures which indicate that the sutras were very popualar one time. The Vashasika system of Kanada finds mention in vedant sutras also which shows that the former were composed earlier to Mahrishi Vayas who is called the author of Vedanta.[3]

In view of the above evidences, it could be concluded that Vaisesika is the oldest of all systems of Vedic Philosphy and was composed by Kanad and it is the first systematic work of Vaisesika Philosophy belonging to 6th century B.C.

REFERENCE

1. तदाप्यहं भविष्यामि सोमशर्मा द्विजोत्तमः।
प्रभासतीर्थमासाद्य योगात्मा लोकविश्रुतः ॥२०२॥
तत्रापि मम न पुत्रा भविष्यन्ति तपोधनाः।
अक्षपादः कणादश्च उलूको वत्स एव च॥२०३॥

— Vayu Purana, Purva, Chapter 23

२. **The word Kanada has been otherwise interpreted by some as meaning Atom-eater, and it is suggested that the author of the Vaisesika-Sutras is called by that name because he has propounded the theory of atoms.**

3. (i) महद् दीर्घवद्वा ह्रस्वपरिमण्डलाभ्याम्।
(ii) उभयथापि न कर्मातस्तदभावः।
(iii) समवायाभ्युपगमाच्च साम्यादनवस्थितेः।
(iv) नित्यमेव च भावात्।
(v) रूपादिमत्त्वाच्च विपर्ययो, दर्शनात्।
(vi) उभयथा च दोषात्।
(vii) अपरिग्रहाच्चात्यन्तमनपेक्षा।

— Veds. 11.2.11-17

4

Atomic Theory of Kanada and Atom Bomb

4

ATOMIC THEORY OF KANADA AND ATOM BOMB

Kanada is the first expounder of atomic theory which is based upon the existence of real things in the universe. The Vaisesika sutra of Kanada consists of 10 books and each book has 2 chapters, the total sutras being 370 as details given below.

Book	I	II	III	IV	V	VI	VII	VIII	IX	X
No. of Sutras	31	31	19	13	18	16	28	6	13	9

The Vaisesika Darsan is one of the well-known six systems of the Vedic philosophy. However, the later development of atomic theory is the product of Nyaya Vaisesika School contributed by Gotama and Kanada.

A number, of commentaries on this system are available. The Prasastapada Bhasya, also known as Padartha-dharmasamggrahs is one of the very well-known books of the

Vaisesika School. Sankara Misra wrote a notable commentary on the Vaisesika known as Upaskara.

ATOMIC THEORY OF KANADA

Kanada has divided the universe under six categories as under –

1. Drayva (substance)
2. Guna (Quality)
3. Karma i.e. action
4. Samanya means belonging or generality or coordination
5. Visesa means particular
6. Sameyaya which relates to the relation to the constituent part.

Kanada has subdivided the substances in to following entities namely :

(i) Earth (ii) Water (iii) Fire or heat (iv) Air (v) Time (vi) Space beside mind and soul.

It may be noted that these substances are not to be taken in their superficial form but in term of their composition. The earth represents all substances which are solid. Similarly water and air will denote liquid and gas substances. These are composed of different kind of parmanus. Akash i.e. ether, dik i.e. space and kala which means time have been mentioned as eternal and prevading and are insperceptible substances. The origin and destruction of objects of the world has been explained through combination and separation of Pramanus.

Parmanu (Atom), according to Kanada is the smallest part of a substance and everything in the universe is made of parmanus, and no further division is possible of a parmanu. In fact, it is the ultimate particle of each of 4 entitled substances earth, fire, water and air. Such a particle is necessarily super sensuous. However, it does not imply its non-existence and it may be due to the action of certain factors which stand in its way of perception. The important characteristics of atoms are:

i. Parmanu is the smallest/ultimate particle of substance of water, air, earth and fire. It is indivisible and in capable of further analysis.

ii. The parmanus of Earth Air, Fire & water have the essential attributes touch taste smell & colour.

iii. There can be no visual perception of Parmanu and sense organs can not percieve them.

iv. They are eternal.

v. They are the ultimate material cause of the universe. Under the action of Teja (Heat) Parmanu, under go chemical change resulting into transformation of characterstics of Parmanu and reunion with different groups and configuration forming a new product with different properties :

The process of chemical change has been examplified by a raw earthen pot put into fire. Under the action of heat its colour, physical properties, strength all under go change and the new product shows different properties.

Similarly in the case of earthen bricks and the bricks burnt and baked in a kiln a wide difference of properties takes place:

Raw Earth Brick (Brittle, Colour, Grey)

Burnt Brick (Tough, Stronger Colour, Pale or red)

Uniting of Parmanus and formation of substances: The occurance of Parmanus and their uniting with each other and forming the substances have been expounded by Kanada as under.

1) Parmanu of a substance unites with another Parmanu to form Dvynuka which could be called molecule. The molecule have the same property as that of the original property of the Parmanu.

2) Parmanus may also unite in a group two, three or four numbers (pairs, triads, teterads etc.)

3) The binary molecules i.e. Dvynukas may unite in pairs or by groups of three, four, five etc.

4) The aggregates thus formed create elementry substances. The qualities and properties of these aggregate Parmanus remain the same as original Parmanus till no chemical change takes place under the action of teja.

Modern Theory of Atom

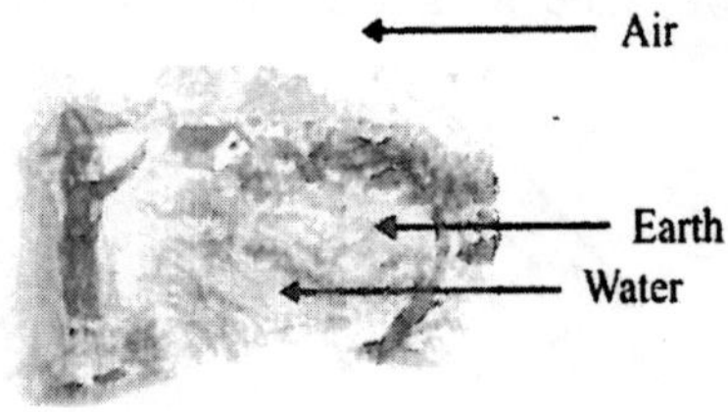

- Everything around us living and non-living, is made up of matter which in made up of molecules. A molecule is the tiniest particle of something that will be just like it.

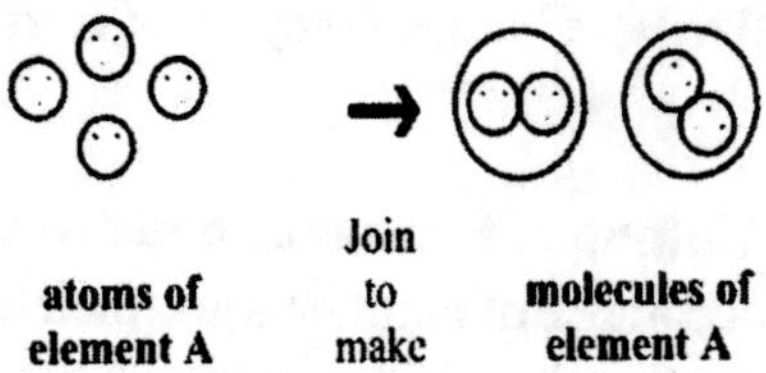

- A molecule is made up of even tinier things called atoms. Just like molecules, atoms can also be different from each other. But while there are millions of different kind of molecules, there are just about a 100 different kinds of atoms.

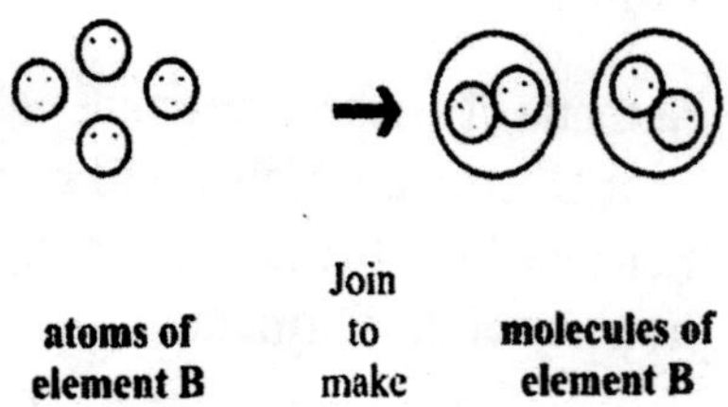

- Some molecules have the same kind of atoms. These molecules join together to make an element. So an element has the same kind of molecules and the same kind of molecules and the same kind of atoms.

- Some molecules have different kinds of atoms. These molecules join together to make a compound. So a compound has the same kind of molecules. But each molecule has more than one kind of atoms

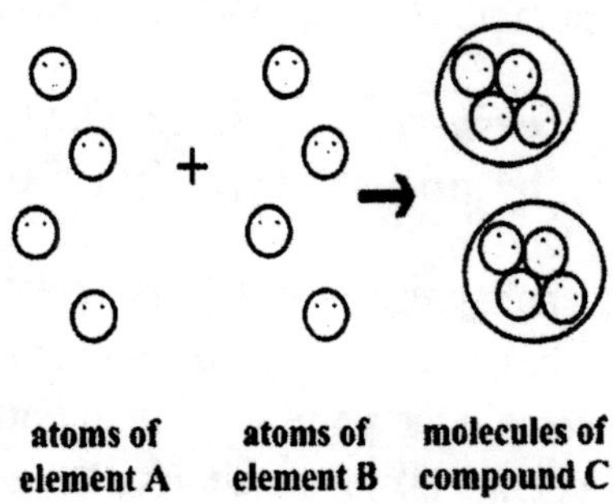

Kanada's Atomic Theory

1. Every thing in the universe is made of Pramanus (Atoms) which is the smallest particle/

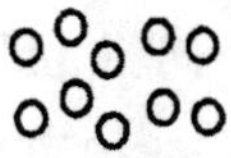

Pramanu

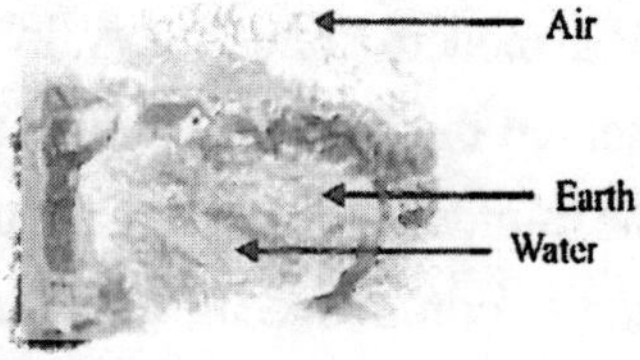

2. An atom meets other atom to form Binary Molecule

3. Atoms of a sublance unite in pairs

Called Dvy nukas or Binary **Molecules**

4. They join with other pairs of atoms or a single atom

(i)

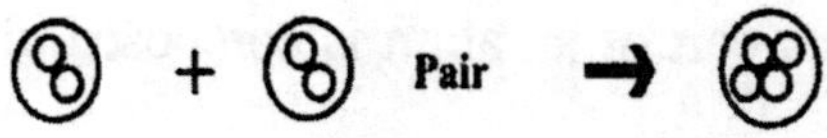

Quaternary

(ii)

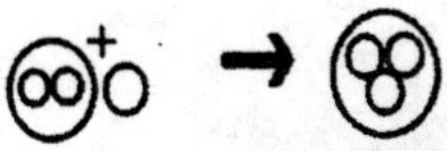

Triade molecule

(iii)

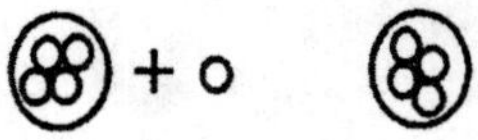

4. Aggregate

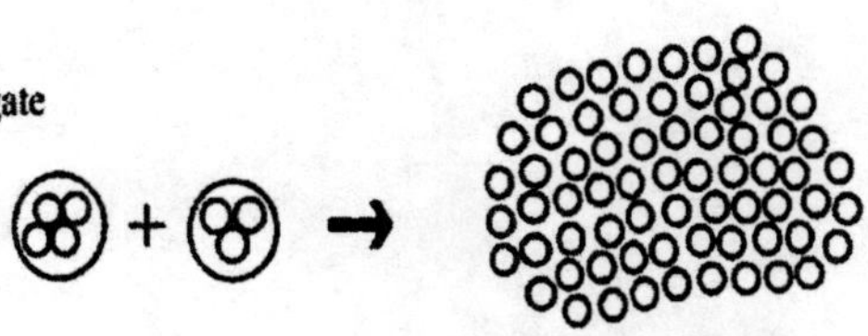

Elementary substance

COMPARISON WITH MODERN ATOMIC THEORY

The Atomic Theory of Kanada holds close comparison with the modern atomic theory. John Dalton, an English chemist, presented the Atomic Theory in the year 1808 and known as the founder of Theory of Atoms. According to this theory, matter is composed of atoms and an atom is the smallest particle of matter which cannot be sub-divided further. Atoms of same element were said to have similar properties like mass, volume. Also that atoms combine in a definite proportion to form compound atoms.

ATOM BOMB

The later research has shown that an atom can be further divided into three parts called electrons, protons, neutrons etc. Protons and neutrons are present in the extra nuclear part. Thus, the nucleus part of an atom is composed of protons and neutrons.

In the year 1938 Frutz Strassman, lise Mather an atto French discovered that uranuim 235 nuclear can be split into smaller elements and that controlled nuclear reaction can be carried out and a very large amount of energy is released splitting heavy atomic nuclear. This resulted into making of Atom Bomb and nuclear power plant.

The Atomic theory of ancient India expounded by Kanada, had research work been carried out further supported with experiements in Laboratory, approperiately conducted and encouragement had been given, perhaps it would also have resulted into making an atom bomb. Albruni - an Arab scholar has rightly commenated:

"For sciences to develop it was necessary that the kings and princes should encourage science and its representatives and they should free the minds of the scholars from the daily anxieties for the necessities of life and stimulate their energies to earn more fame an favour, the yearning for which is the pith and marrow of human nature. The present times (in India), however, are not of this king. They are very opposite and therefore, it is quite impossible that a new science or any new kind of research should arise in our day. What we have of sciences is nothing but the scanty remains of by gone better times".

Alberuni further comments :

"Mahmud utterly ruined the propserity of the country and performed there wonderful exploits by which the Hindus became atoms of dust scattered in all directions and like a tale of old. This is the reason why Hindu sciences have retired far away from those parts of the country conquered by us and have fled to places where our hands yet cannot reach."

REFERRENCE

1. अथैकादशक्षणा। वह्निोदनाभिघातान्यतरेण द्व्यणुकारम्भकपरमाणौ कर्म ततो विभागस्ततो द्रव्यारम्भक संयोगनाशस्ततो द्व्यणुकनाशः ताते द्व्यणुकनाशविशिष्टं कालमपेक्ष्य विभागजविभागस्ततः पूर्वसंयोगनाशस्तत उत्तरसंयोगस्ततः परमाणुकर्मनाशस्तदनन्तर-मद्दृष्टवदात्मसंयोगात् तत्रैव परमाणौ द्रव्यारम्भानुगुणा क्रिया ततो विभागस्ततः पूर्वसंयोगनाशस्ततो द्रव्यारम्भकसंयोगस्ततो द्व्यणुकोत्पत्तिस्ततो रक्ताद्युत्पत्तिरित्येकादशक्षणा।

—K.R., p.23

5

Missiles Bombs & Canon

5

MISSILES, BOMBS AND CANON

A missile has been defined as a rocket propelled weapon often with a nuclear warhead projected, or discharged through the air.

New Agni-I Variant Missile range 700 km

India has successfully developed short range, medium range and long range missiles of 150 Km, 700 Km. & 3000 Km. i.e. Agni I & Variant of Agni I & Agni III, besides Prithvi & Dhanusha. Other advanced countries have also developed all ranges of missiles including inter continental one.

Missiles in Ancient India will surprise many a one. However, the extensive study of ancient scriptures reveals that missiles in primal form were employed in war and were fitted with bows (Dhanusha). Braham Astra was one such missile which was used by Indrajit (Meghnad) the son of Ravana as mentioned in Sunder Kanda in Ramayana by Valmiki.[1] The use of the following kind of missiles[2] have also been mentioned :

1) Missile inducing sleep.
2) Missile that induces yawning.
3) Missile that inebriates the person against whom it is directed.
4) Missiles that severly torments by heating and melts the object aimed at etc.

Similarly in Mahabharta period the use of missiles in battle was made, and it was a part of training of Dharrurveda. In fact the entire military science and art of the Mahabbarta age seem to have been comprehended by the generic term Dhanurveda, the dhanu or bow being regarded as the type or symbol of all weapons or methods of warfare. Thus the Dhannrveda or the general science of weapons and warfare is mentioned in different references as conveying different kinds of military knowledge or accomplishments.

One passage [i, I39,6,I7] extends the scope of Dhanurveda so as to include the knowledge of fighting with all weapons of which the bow is a mere type, viz. fighting with club, sword, car, bow, arrow, and missiles. Also the study of the Dhanurveda is to be principally by practice is also shown

from the case of Arjuna who goes out and precision oven at night and thus becomes an expert in the various military arts such as those connected with the management of horses, elephants, and the like [i, 132, 28]. The technology of fabricating missiles appears to be primal one and perhaps missiles were mostly fitted with bows.

BOMB AND CANON

A Bomb is defined as an explosive device triggered by impact or a timer dropped from the air thrown or placed by hand. In ancient India no reference on use of bomb is available. However the use of Canon & artillery was there from the early medieval India and it was medieval India that the use of Guns, Cannon and the of throwing was used and became a common phenomenon in all the wars fought after 1370 A.D.

Historians hold different views in regard to the use of gun, cannon for the first time in India. According to the some of them the guns, cannon were used during the time of Iltutmish (1200-36 A.D.). Similarly Busani has been quoted to show that the Cannon were used during the siege of Ranthmbhor (1299-1300 A.D.). However these views has been refuted by the many other historians on various grounds and there is no convincing evidence that guns and cannon were used in 13th Century.

The first convincing evidence that the use of artillary in India is the battle which was fought between Raja of Vijaya Nagara and Mohammad Shah Bahmaru wherein Bahmani King is reported to have collected a train of artillary which had never till then been employed by the muslims in the Deccan, he gave the command to Mookurrib Khan, son of Sufdur Khhan Seestany attaching to him a number of Toorks and Europeans ecquainted with the ins and out of Gunnary. Firishta informs us that in the next battle with Vijaya Nagar about eight months later Muqurrab Khan used his artillary with great effect. Hence-forth the artillary formed an important weapon in the wars of Deccan.

The use of artillary came forth in between Sixtinth century. Bahadur Shah (Gujrat) was having a good store of Cannon. Rumi Khan had brought with him a big cannon known as Egyption Cannon. It is said that it was drawn by 300 men and innumerable buffaloes. It was made in Egypt in 937 (A.D.1530). Nadvi also cites many other instances of the use of guns in India before Babar employed them in the first battle of Panipat in A.D. 1526. Babar says that the soldiers in Bengal were expert artillarists.

REFERRENCES ON GUNS & ARTILLARY

1. Quran, III. 102; XIII, 38 etc.
2. Ibid, V.2
3. I.H. Qureshi Administration of the Sultanate of Delhi, P.22-23.
4. Imam means a leader and Khalifah, successor, so called because he succeeded the Prophet in his secular authority.
5. W.Mirza Kulliyat-i-Hasan Sajzi, e.g. P.488 Life and Works of Amir Khurov, P.124.
6. Burani P. 491-92

6

Wars and Weapons In Ancient India

6

WAR WEAPONS IN ANCIENT INDIA

Modern War

Modern war is a hi-tech affair and is planned carefully in conjunction with not only infantry and artillery but other divisions of the army like corpse of engineers , medical corpse, signal corpse etc. are all mobilized simultaneously to fight the war.

There is almost no direct confrontation between the two sides fighting each other and the entire exercise is under the veil of hillock, trenches, bushes etc. Darkness or night is regarded as the best time of fighting.

The weapons of war are automatic guns, riffles, artillery mortar, shelling, mines, and blasting rockets, missiles with or without nuclear war heads to strike at the target point hundred of miles away. As the war esculates, Air force is deployed for dropping bombs and also soldiers at a far off place with the help of parachutes. In case of coastal towns or cities approachable by sea routes the coastal guards or the Navy is also called upon to backup the ground war.

The ancient warswere simple affairs, freefrom such cumbersome paraphernalia but more frequent between two neighboring kingdoms or monarchies The casualties were, however, much more

Modern Weapons of War

ANCIENT WEAPONS

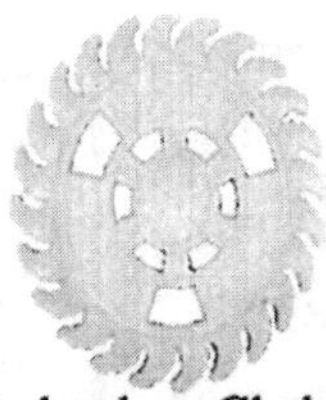

Sudarshan Chakra

Axe

Mace

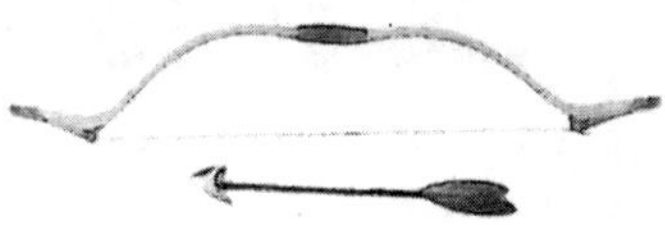

Bow & Arrow

Trishul(Three edged spear)

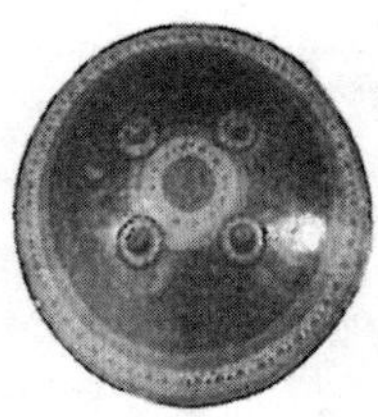

Shield

Sword

Spear

Musal

not only of human life but animal force like horses , elephants etc. Medical facilities for removal / treatment of injured soldiers were rather inadequate, so much so that the battle field was littered with dead bodies of men and animals and blood shedding. In the famous Kalinga war wherein over1 lakh of people were slain the blood had been flowing like rain water, as mentioned by some historians.

WARS AND WEAPONS IN VEDIC INDIA

Aryans had to fight several battles to establish themselves and to spread their civilization necessitating warfare for a long period. There is mention of forts in Rig-Veda and also numerous instances in other Vedas to this effect. Rig-Veda refers to the blockade of 100 cities of non Aryana by Rijasvan in his fight against Krishna Garbhan dusky complexion of people. Similarly Rig-Veda IV, 30.21 mentions like killing of 30,000 Dasas.

In other passage of Rig-Veda (X, 22, 8) there is a prayer to Indra" *O destroyer of foes kill them. Destroy the Dasa race ". We are surrounded on all sidesby Dasyu tribe.*

Chariots have always attracted Aryans in peace and war, fabrication of chariots comprising of wheels, their main body and roof was an industry. The occupation like carpentry and metal working find mention in Rig-Veda which were used for making/fabricating chariots. The chariots were driven by horses and in peace time chariot races were organized and in wars, they were the most common vehicles for fighting battles.

During war, the royal priest[4] accompanied the king in battle and recited prayers for victory in the war. The common weapons of war were bows, arrows and swords made of metal, copper and later of iron. The King or chiefTon would cover his main body with protective layers to safeguard himself from the piercing arrows. The following hymns of Rig-Veda addressed to arms prove the above pattern for fighting wars. [1]*"These two [the bow tips] who go forward like a woman going to a rendezvous, hold the arrow in their lap as a mother holds a son. Let the two bow tips, working together, pierce our enemies and scatter our foes.*

He [the quiver which holds the arrows] is the father of many daughters [arrows]. He makes a rattling sound as he goes down into battle. The quiver wins the attacks and all the skirmishes when he is strapped on a back and set to work.

Standing in the chariot, the skillful chatioteer drives his prize-winning horses forward wherever he wishes to go. Praise the power of the reins: the guides follow the mind that is behind them.

Neighing violently, the horses with their showering hoofs outstrip everyone with their chariots. Trampling down the foes with the tips of their hoofs, they destroy their enemies without veering away.

Spare us, 0 weapons flying true to its mark;let our body be stone. Let Soma speak a blessing upon us;let Aditi give us shelter".

Bows, arrows and chariots driven by horses remained the essential part of war during the Vedic period besides spears and spades and swords.

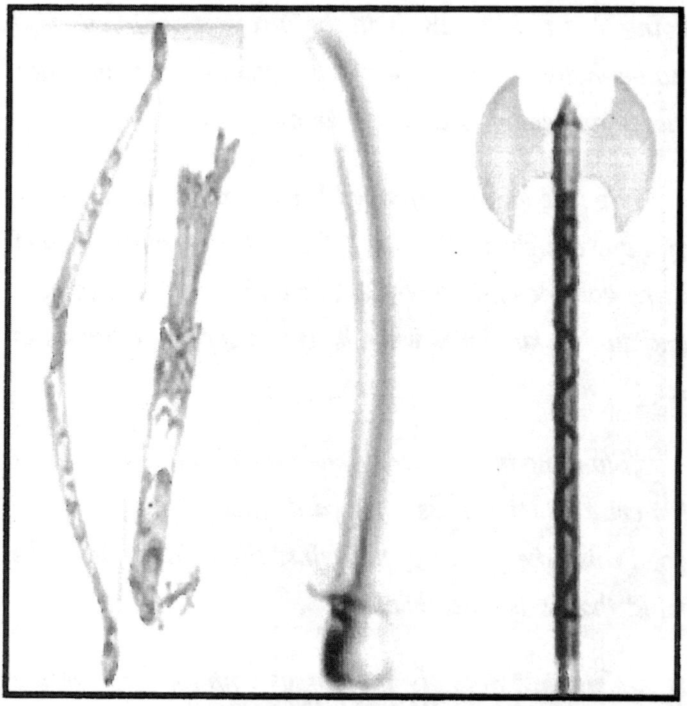

Weapons of War During Vedic Period

LATER VEDIC PERIOD

The later Vedic period saw great advancement in the material life of people and also the political changes. The small kingdoms expanded their territories toform a bigger political entity and a tendency to annex more territories by the kings and monarchs was evinced.The famous war of Mahabharata between Kaurvas and Pandavas over the matter of territory was per haps fought during this period around 950 BC.

During later Vedic times, the weapons of war remained almost the same mainly bows, arrows, spears, swords and mace. However, there was marked advance ment in the quality and technique of fabricating them. The bows were heavier and the arrows were sharper to hit the target with much more force and some times were named after deities with divine blessings. Mahabharata mentions of blessing Arjuna by Lord Shiva and providing him some divine bows and arrows. Comprehensive train ing in the science and art of archery was considered essential for a prince or king. Even expertise in Dhanurveda assumed a marriage qualification & the valour of a king was tested through his competency in

Dhanur veda i.e. Archery. The essential condition of wedding Draupadi was hitting the eye of a revolving fish through an arrow only by seeing its shadow in the oil tank which was satisfied by Arjuna resulting into the marriage.Ramayana also mentions that the condition stipulated for marriage of Sita was that whosoever would lift the 'Shiv dhanusha' would marry Sita, which was regarded as a heroic deed of valor during this period. The quality of chariots improvised and driving of a chariot i.e. charioteering became a respectful profession. Shri Krishna during the famous Mahabharata war accepted the role of a charioteer to drive the chariot of Arjuna. The war would start with blowing of couch shell and followed by beating drums and sounding of horns, biguls etc. The famous Mahabharata war believed to have been fought during latter Vedic period has been described under :-

The War Would Begin With Blowing of Shell

"At holy plains of Kurukshetra the armies of Kaurvas and pandavas were stationed confronting each other. The armies comprising of chariots driven by horses, foot soldiers armed with bows and arrows stood in an array quite ready to start fighting. The great Bhishma pitamaha was appoited as chief commander by Duryodhana for the war of the day. On Pandava side Bheem was to lead the army. The reputed warriors were stationed as strategic points. The most renowned warrior and the top bow man Arjuna was sitting in the chariot armored with his famous 'Gandeev Dhamesh' & the chariot driven by white horses while the Charioteering was done by Shri Krishna.

To begin with *Bhishma Pitamaha* the commander of the army blew couch shell with high volume followed by sounding of biguls and horns, beating of drums to excite the army. On Pandava's side Arjuna inturn also blew couch shell named 'Dev dutta'. Sri Krishna blew the couch shell named as 'panchjanya'. The tumulous and fearful sound had shaken the earth."

This also speaks the pattern of war during later Vedic period as the incident of Mahabharata is believed to have happened during this period. The weapons of war which find mention in Mahabharata are as under:

(i) Club fighting

(ii) Sword wielding

(iii) Archery

(iv) Spear throwing

(v) Fighting with missiles

(vi) Seizing weapons

(vii) Rathsiksha i.e. the skill whereby the warrior learnt the art of circling with his war car of doubling and returning the skill of avoiding being made a viratha (deprived of one's war car) and preventing it from being splintered into fragments by the attack of the enemy.

The military was organized in patrols and battalion.

It is interesting to note that the mace blow was common during Mahabharata war and Durodhana - the Kaurva head was killed by Bheema by mace blows.

ANCIENT INDIA (600 BC - 700 AD)

The following important wars fought after 600 B.C. in ancient India are as mentioned under:-

1. Conquest wars fought by the Magadha rulers e.g. Bhimbsara, Ajat shatru.
2. War of Alexender with King Porhuosh fought at North West India, now in Pakistan.
3. War fought by Nanda King to capture Magdha.
4. War fought by Chandragupta Maurya to defeat Nanda Kings.
5. Famous Kalinga war by Ashoka.
6. Series of conquest wars by Harshwardhana.

In all these notable wars the military was organized into under mentioned divisions, however during the period of Chandragupta and there after where the territory of the empire covered almost the whole India, including vast sea coast, on eastern, southern and western frontiers two more divisions were added e.g. Navy and transport division to facilitate the essential supply to army.

1. Elephant Division
2. Cavalry Division
3. Infantry Division
4. Chariot Division

The elephant division was in the fore front at the time of war to storm and break the fortresses mostly situated in hilly areas and to make out the communication line for the infantry and chariot division as there were no roads during those days. Also at the time of direct confrontation with enemy the elephant division will storm the army of enemy with trampling. The warriorsseated on the back of elephant would be equipped with blows and arrows to hit the enemy soldiers. The strength of elephants in Chandragupta army was as high as 9,000 and in case of Nanda it was around 6,000 elephants.

A War Elephant

Cavalry Division was another important division and the soldiers would be equipped with spears and swords to hit the enemy soldiers. India has a legacy in metal casting technology as well as steel. As such the quality of swords and spears was an important factor for the lethal power of these weapons. The strength of Cavalry division in case of Nanda kings was around 20,000 and in case of Chandragupta Maurya it was around 30,000.

The Chariot Division was especially meant for the warriors who were expert in archery with a good training and practice and the warriors therein would be equipped with arrows and bows. It is said that reason of success of Ajat shatru had been that he attached a special mechanical device with his chariot by fixing a special 'musal' a thick iron rod and it was rotating with a largesweep while the chariot was moving and would keep the enemy away from chariot. The craftsman fabrication the chariots were very expert in their job. As such the production / fabrication of chariots was a big industry in Ancient India. The horse chariots were however losing their importance not only in north-east but also in north-west India, where they had been introduced by the Vedic people. Very few elephants were maintained by the rulers of the States in north-west India, though some of them maintained as many horses as the Magadhan King did. The possession of numerous elephants gave an edge to the Magadhan princes.

Chariot Drivers by 4 horses

Infantry Division was the largest one. Chandragupta Maurya has 4 lakh foot soldiers in the army. They were the people to surround the enemy forces and were equipped with spears to hit the enemy from a distance.

WEAPONS OF WAR

1. Sword Wielding
2. Archery- Bow and Arrows
3. Spear throwing

AGE OF GUNS AND CANONS

Guns and cannons were used during the period of Ellutmish (1200-36 AD) for the first time and become a common phenomena in all the wars fought after 1500 AD.

CANNONS AND ROCKETS IN INDIA

According to a publication of National Science Centre, Govt. of India, adopting European and Ottoman knowledge fabricating of canons in India, occurred during early 16th Century, Besides the Iron cannons, Bronze Cannons, Bronze Cannons, Forge-welded Cannons and Composite type Cannons were also common in India. A writeup of National Science Centre Delhi mentions -

"Important Indian Innovations in cannon tecnology include the Shaturnal, Multipiece screwable Cannons, Yarghu (the Multibarrel cannon cleaner) etc. Indian innovations in cannon technology like shaturnal (cannons fired from back of camels), composite cannons (of inner wrought iron bore and outer bronze casting) and bans

(battlefield rockets) offer sufficient proof of Indian ingenuity in this technology. Tipu Sultan was the first to apply scientific principles to test and perfect rocket and missile technology. Some of the rocket fired by Tipu's men are preserved in the Artillery Museum at Woolwich in London".

DIVINE WEAPONS IN ANCIENT INDIA 'SUDARSHAN CHAKRA'

Apart from the common weaponry, deployed in ancient India, a divine weapon which figures frequently in Hindu scriptures, is a revolving wheel (Sudarshan Chakra).

This is the weapon which Lord Vishnu is shown holding in one of his fingers. Shri Krishna the incarnate of Lord Vishnu is also mentioned in puranas as holding the Sudarshan Chakra in one of his fingers. Though normally shown with playing flute, there are situations where Shri Krishna does hold the Sudarshan chakra also. Mahabharata mentions 'Rajyasuya'yajna performed by Yudhishtra after his coronation where in all the kings and princes of the region were invited and Shri Krishna was appointed as the head Priest of the yajna. This was whemently opposed by Shishupala, one of the kings who abused and called names again and again, an act of gross insult which no body would tolerate and after abusing and calling names 100 times, Shri Krishna held his sudarshan chakra (revolving wheel) at his finger & beheaded Shishupala so quickly and briskly. This shows the lethal force of the weapon.

What was this revolving wheel or sudarshan charka? Was it a figment of imagination or reality? only research scholars can decide. However a wheel revolving on a finger and with cutting edge in feasible working on the principle of Fly wheel. According to a senior professor of mechanical engineering of IIT Delhi, such a wheel must be of light weight and of steel grade metal and frictionless. The wheel could work on the prin-ciple of first law of motion of Newton called as father of science. The first law of motion is described as under:

Any thing moving in straight line will go on moving unless some resisting force is applied to it. This means that a moving vehicle should go on moving and would come to stop only on account of the frictional force between the road and the tyres. Therefore if the moving wheel is made frictionless, a little jerk by the finger would keep the wheel rotating like fly wheel and the sharp cutting edge at the rim of the wheel may tear and shear the person to be attacked .However there is no mention of this weapon anywhere else except that of Lord Vishnu or Shri Krishna or the goddess Durga.

REFERRENCES

1. Rig Veda samhita 6.75.

2. Mahabharata - Shrimad Bhagvad Geeta.

धर्मक्षेत्रे कुरुक्षेत्रे समवेता युयुत्सवः।
मामकाः पाण्डवाश्चैव किमकुर्वत सञ्जय॥१॥

दृष्ट्वा तु पाण्डवानीकं व्यूढं दुर्योधनस्तदा।
आचार्यमुपसङ्गम्य राजा वचनमब्रवीत!॥२॥

पश्यैतां पाण्डुपुत्राणामाचार्य महतीं चमूम्।
व्यूढां द्रुपदपुत्रेण तव शिष्येण धीमता॥३॥

अपर्याप्तं तदस्माकं बलं भीष्माभिरक्षितम्।
पर्याप्तं त्विदमेतेषां बलं भीमाभिरक्षितम्॥१०॥

तस्य सञ्जनयन्हर्षं कुरुवृद्धः पितामहः।
सिंहनादं विनद्योच्चैः शङ्खं दध्मौ प्रतापवान्॥१२॥

ततः शङ्खांश्च भेर्यश्च पणवानकगोमुखाः।
सहसैवाभ्यहन्यन्त स शब्दस्तुमुलोऽभवत्॥१३॥

ततः श्वेतैर्हयैर्युक्ते महति स्यन्दने स्थितो।
माधवः पाण्डवश्चैव दिव्यौ शङ्खौ प्रदध्मतुः॥१४॥

—Srimad Bhagwad Geeta 1.1-14

3. **Ancient India,** R.S. Sharma NCERT Publication.
4. **History of Ancient & Early Medeaval India -** Dr. Upender Singh.

Eminent Scientists of Ancient India

7

Baudhayana

The First Great Geometer

7

BAUDHAYANA THE FIRST GREAT GEOMETER

Baudhayana (8th century B.C.) is considered to be the great geometer of ancient India. The science of geometry in ancient India developed with the yajnas or fire sacrifice which necessiated the construction of altars in Vedic civilization. In fact the whole culture and civilization of this land developed in ancient times owe their origin to yajnas. Altars were constructed to perform many kinds of Vedic sacrifices which were of two classes: (i) Nitya and (ii) Kamya. The Kamya sacrifices were performed with special motives and as per strict injunction laid-down. Such sacrifice must be performed in a altar of prescribed shape or size. It was the general belief of Aryans that even a slight irregularity in shape was enough to nullify the object of the whole ritual, therefore, necessiating the extra care in regard to the shape and size of the altar.

We have Sulbas or Sulba Sutras which are the works of several preceptors and are the manuals of construction of altaras. Out of all the Sulbas or Sulba Sutras, Baudhayana is the latest and biggest, and was composed by Baudhayana between 500-300 B.C. It is divided into 3 chapters. The first chapter contains 116 Sutras (aphorisms) of which the opening two are merely introductory; Sutras 3-21 define the various measures ordinarily employed in the Sulbas; Sutras 22-62 give the more important of the geometrical propositions necessary for the construction of the sacrificial altars; and Sutras 63-113 deal briefly with the relative positions and spatial magnitudes of the various Vedis (or altars).

The second chapter of the Baudhayana Sulba Sutra consists of 83 Sutras of which the major portion, Sutras 1-61 are devoted to the description of the special relations in the different constructions of the Agnis (or the large Fire altars made of bricks) in general, and the remaining portion, Sutras 62-83, elaborates the construction of the two simplest Agnis (The Garhapatyaciti or the House-holders, Fire-altar and Chandas-citi or the verse-altar, i.e., the Agni made, as it were ,or mantras instead of bricks). The third chapter contains altogether 323 Sutras and described the construction of as may as 17 different kinds of Kamya Agnis (or the altars for the sacrifices performed with a view to attain definite objects) of rather complex nature. In some cases, the descriptions by Baudhayana are quite elaborate, whereas at many other places they are brief and merely indicative.

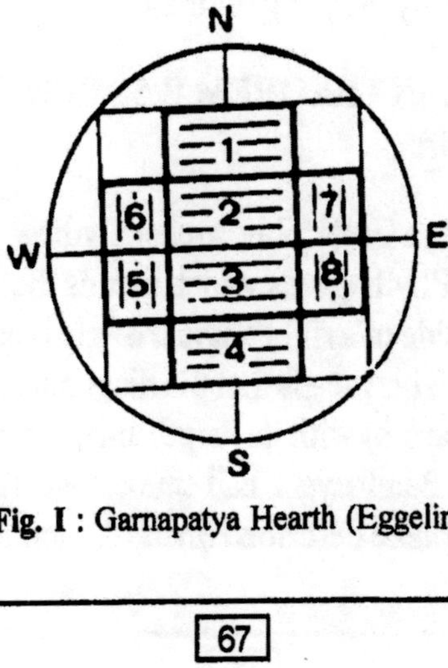

Fig. I : Garnapatya Hearth (Eggeling)

Baudhayana while describing the construction of various altars, deals with a number. of postulates in connection with the division of figures such as straight lines, rectangle, circle and triangle. These are real signs of geometrical operation. These postulates include :-

I. Dividing a circle into a number of parts.
II. Bisecting the diagonal of a rectangle.
III. To show that the diagonals of a rhombus bisects each other at right angle.
IV. Dividing a triangle into a number of equal similar parts.
V. Constructing a parallelogram at rectangle on same base and within the same parallel to show the equality of area etc.

In case of the Baudhyana sutra, there is a reference that Dhisnya be a sphere of circle in shape and it is divided into 9 equal parts. When it is circular, it describes a small circle above the centre and the annuals into 8 equal parts by dividing in diameters etc. This is nothing but dividing a circle into a number of parts by drawing diameters.

PYTHEGOREAN THEOREM WAS DISCOVERED BY BAUDHAYANA

Known after a Greek philosopher, Pythagoras (540 B.C.) the theorem of Phythagoras which means that the sphere of each rectangle side of a right angle triangle is equal to sphere of the diagonal. This means that the diagonal of the rectangle produces both (areas) with its length and produce separately. This is what the Baudhayana had enunciated. This means that the area of the sphere described on the diagonal of the sphere

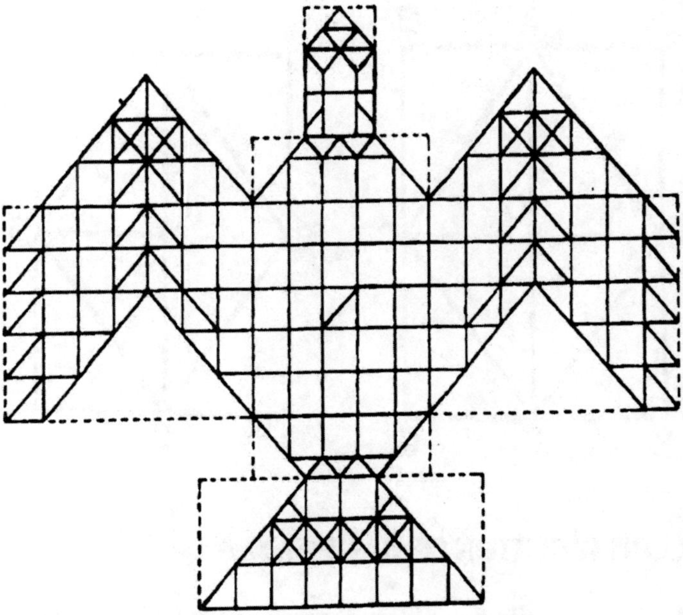

Fig. 2 : Caturasra Syena-cit.

is double the area of that square. Baudhyana theorem of sphere of diagonal is well illustrated in the construction of the KATURASRA SYENA-CIT as discovered by Burk. Caturasra Syena-Cit is very notable Fire-altar of the shape of falcon with curved wings and out spread tail the details of which have been given in Baudhayana Sulbha Sutra (translated by Thihant). The altar utilizes 200 bricks in all.

The sphere ACFE on the diagonal AC of the sphere ABCD of the four sphere forming the atman of this altar is obviously equal to the sphere EADEH on the side AD and sphere DGEH on the side DC.

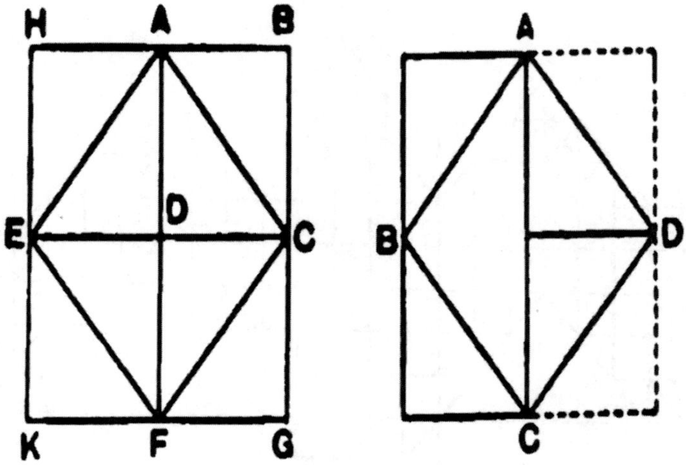

CONTRIBUTION OF BAUDHAYANA

The contribution of Baudhayana as a great geometer of ancient India is very significant. The pythagaurus theorem as square of diagonals goes to his credit and infact it should be rightly called as Baudhayana theorem as it was he who demonstrated the truth for the first time and gave its application. Baudhayana has not given the proof of the theorem. However, we join with Trihaut in the following words.

"The authors of the Sutras do not give us any hint as to the way in which they found their proposition regarding the diagonal of a square, but we suppose that they, too, were observant of the fact that the square of the diagonal is divided by its own diagonals into four triangles one of which is equal to half the first square. This is at the same time an immediately convincing proof of the Pythagorean proposition as far as squares or equilateral rectangular triangles are concerned".

As has already been mentioned, the science of geometry developed around the yajnas in construction of Vedis of various shapes. As such the development of the geometry took place here without having been borrowed from other countries. Following is the brief of contribution of Baudhayana to the science of geometry :

I. To give postulates of geometrical construction comprising of various geomertrical operations.

II. To discover the theorem of square of the diagonal called as Pythagaurus Theorem.

III. To determine accurately the value of under root 2 and to give the concept of irrationality of construction.

It may however, be mentioned that Baudhayana was not the first to discover all the geometrical concepts mentioned in his SULBA SUTRA and surely Rigveda, Taiteeraya Sanhita and Satpatha Brahmna have provided the same guidance to the matter but it is sure that he was a great teacher. He was the first teacher whose writings have influenced many Acharyas of Ancient India for centuries like Apastamba, Katyayana, Manu etc.

8

Susurta
The Father of Surgery

8

SUSURTA
THE FATHER OF SURGERY

"In both branches of the Aryan stock, surgical practice (as well as medical) reached a high degree of perfection at a very early period."

Encyclopaedia Britannica
by Chales Creighton.

"The whole plastic surgery in Europe took a new flight when these cunning devices of Indian workmen became known to us."

Dr. Hirschberg of Berlin.

These are the compliments made by international authorities on ancient Indian surgery for which the credit goes to Susruta who is regarded as father of ancient Indian surgery.

Susruta lived somewhere in 6th century B.C. It was he, who from scanty material created science of surgery in methodical order inviting the admiration of the world even after thousands of years of human history of surgery known as 'Susruta shalya Tantra' composed around 6th century B.C. which contains a systematic account of the surgical experiences of old surgeons by collecting the scattered facts of the science from the vast range of the vedic literature.

DEVELOPMENT OF SURGERY IN ANCIENT INDIA :

Surgery like many other sciences developed around the yajna i.e. fire sacrifice. It was Susurta who first classified all surgical operations into eight different kinds and grouped them under various heads and yajna became a centre of anatomical surgery.

Before the age of Susurta neither physician nor the surgeon were beholden in great respect and physicians had to go out into the eopen streets calling out the patients like hawkers. As regards surgery they were considered as second to the physicians. In fact, origin of surgery, was the result of the necessity when the arrows piercing into the bodies of warriors had to be taken out. We find mention of the amputation of legs of warriors. During peace time surgery became necessary for the cases of accidents and for the injuries sustained by the rich and poor.

Susruta was not only the surgeon of versatile personality, but he was a teacher of surgical instrument technology as well as metallurgy.

BIRTH AND IDENTITY OF SUSURTA

Susurta has been mentioned to be the son of Vishwamitra the great sage of vedic period though being Akshtray king he rose to the divine level of Rishi. Mahabharta mentions the name of several sons of Vishwamitra which includes Susurta also. It appears that Vishwamitra while foresaking his kingdom and devoting himself in tapsya sent his son Susurta to a high learned king Diyodas for being imparted the knowledge of Ayurveda.

AGE OF SUSURTA SANHITA

It is difficult to ascertain the age of Susurta Sanhita as the original book is not available to us at present. We have only a revised version made by Nagarjuna, an eminent Buddhist philosopher as well as medical scientist. According to some of the authorities (Hass and John Willson) Susurta Sanhita was written much after Mahabharta and the consensus of western opinion is to place NagaArjuna in the first quarter of 300 B.C. and the final recession of Sanhita by NagaArjuna thereafter. In view of the fact that Susurta has been mentioned by Katyana (400 B.C.) in his work Vartika, the original Sanhita was written before the birth of Lord Buddha.

ACHIEVEMENTS OF SUSURTA

SURGERY

Susurta devoted his life for the cause and performance of surgery and his achievements could be briefed as under:

1. Pre-requisites for performing surgery procedure and new modern techniques.

2. Plastic Surgery and Modern Technique. Performing surgery like amputation, fracture, Harnia, rupture and other such operations with sophiscated techniques.
3. Ophthalmic surgery.
4. Midwifery.
5. Details of instruction in anatomy and surgery.
6. Management and pre-requisite in surgery.

1. **Surgery Procedure** - Susruta laid down the details regarding management of patients before surgery, requirements of operation room etc. As per Susurta-Sanhita if surgery is to be performed in mouth, patient should be kept on fasting and for abdominal surgery, a light refreshment should be given. For operation room, antiseptic treatment should be given and the chamber should be falugated with the vapours of white mastard, nimha leaves etc. He even devised a method of anaesthesia.

2. **Plastic Surgery and modern technique** - The achievements in case of plastic surgery are wonderful. The transplantation of sensible skin flesh by mending it clipt earloped with a patch of sensible skin, skinflex from somewhere the part of the body were the devices which were not even known to the modern plastic surgery for quite long time back and perhaps the method devised by Susruta have influenced the modern surgery *to adopt* the same with usual refixed units and amendments. He described a method for fixing a neve new where it had been cut off.

3. **Amputation and abdominal operations** :- Susruta evolved a wonderful method of joining the intestinal wombs by letting big ants bite the cut ends of the intestines which had been brought nearer to head and then cutting off the body of the ants leaving only the heads of the ants which acts a clamp and well tolerated by the body. In fact it serves the purpose of animal tissue which the modern surgery uses. This method was later on followed by the Arabs and other countries. In warfare which was fought with arrows, Susruta mentioned the use of certain medical plasters to be applied to localise the sharp arrows and thereby identifying the exact location of embedding of arrows. For amputation of limbs the necessity of aneathesetic drugs was realized and wine was used to serve the purpose.

4. **Difficult surgical Operations**: - Susruta performed all types of the operation like fracture, dislocation, harnia, fisstula, removal of foreign bodies etc. involving excision, incision, puncture and other such processes.

5. The genius and surgery skill of Susruta becomes crystal clear in the field of midwifery. Susrutasanhita describes the handling and applications of forceps besides attempting, turning, flexing and glidding movements.

He also tried the caesareass operation in hopeless cases where the maternal passage is not compatible to the child. The requirements of the labour room in the absence of hospital were also prescribed.

6. **Instructions in Practical Surgery and Anatomy: -** Susruta laid down the procedure and method to pursue the study of practical surgery and practical Anatomy, he mentions that a learner should try the knives first on virtual and artificial objects, and how the bandaging is to be learnt etc. For study of practical anatomy the sacrificial animals in yajnas were to be used for the purpose which was perhaps permissible in those days.

Susruta is in favour of 300 bones against 360 bones recognised by vedic traditions. Of those 120 are found in the fore extremities, 170 in the palmist, side back, chest abdomn etc. and rest in the region of neck. It is where the Susurt Sanhita contains anomaly and this may be on account of the fact that the original Susurtsanhita has passed through several recensions. However, the Susurtsanhita has described the union of bones and ligaments nerves, brawins etc. in a wonderful and correct manner.

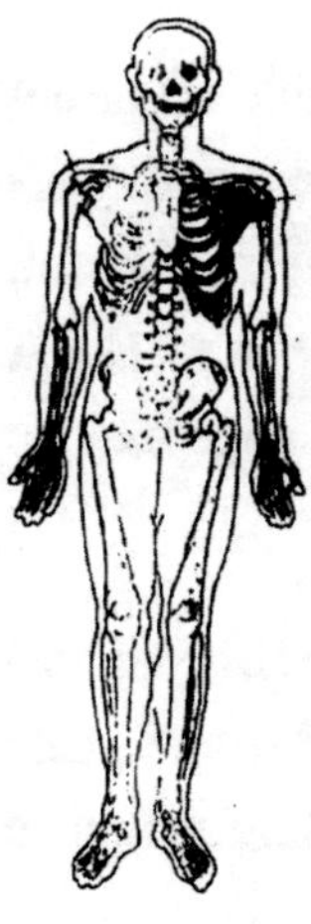

Susruta as surgical instrument technologist : In modern surgery surgeons are only aware with the use and handling of surgical instruments during the performance of operation and they are not concerned with the metallurgy, manufacturing and other requirements which is a job of technologist. Susruta describes more than 100 surgical instruments made of steel and the composition of the metal has also been given. The requirement of these instruments have been mentioned that they should have good handles and firm joints, be well polished, and sharp enough to divide a hair. They should be perfectly clean, and kept in flannel in a wooden box. They included various wshapes of scalpels, bistouries, lancets, scarifiers was, bone-nippers, sciessors, trocars, and needles. There were also blunt hooks, loops, probes (including a caustic holder), directors, sounds, scoops, and forceps (for polypi etc.), as well as catheters, syringes, a rectal speculum and bougies.

The following description on surgical instrument will show that Susruta was possessed of deep knowledge of metallurgy and instrument technology :

"Instruments that are fitted with handles of easy grip and are made of good and pure iron, well-sharp, and are set with edges that are not jagged and end in well-formed points or tops, should be deemed as the best of their kind."

Curvature, bluntness (kuntha-Lit : incapable of cutting hair), unequal sharpness of the edge, roughness and over-shortness are the defective traits in a surgical instrument. Those possessed of contrary features should be used. But A Karapatram set with a very rough (dentated) edge may be used for the purpose of sawing the bones.

A surgical instrument meant for excision (Bhedanam) should be set with an edge as thin as that of a Masura pulse (lentill seed), while an instrument used in scraping should be set with an edge half as thin as that of the former. An instrument used either in connection with the measures of secretion or cutting by uplifting (Vyadhanam) should be set with an edge as fine as the human hair, while an instrument of incision should have an edge half as that of the former.

Surgical instruments should be tempered with one of the tree substances such as alkali, water, and oil. Instruments used in cutting an arrow, a bone or any foreign matter (salyam) pricked into the human body should be tempered with alkali, whereas those that are used in cutting, cleaving and lopping off the flesh from an affected part, should be tempered with water . Instruments used in opening (Vyuadhanam) a vain (sira) or in cutting open a nerve (snayu) should be tempered with oil and should be whetted upon a species of stone slab resembling a Masa pulse in colour, and their set-edge should be protected by putting it in a sheatmade of Salmal i wood.

An instrument, well-shaped, fitted with a convenient handle and capable of (literally) spliting a hair in two and made according to measures laid down in the Sastras, should be alone used in a surgical operation.

SUSURTA - AS TEACHER

Susruta not only practised surgery but taught surgery as well. The pupil who received training in surgery as apprentices must have become good surgeon later on. The adequate material contained in Susruta is a clear testimony to support the fact. Susruta asked their students to try their knives repeatedly first on certain virtual as well as artificial objects before undertaking the actual operation and vegetables were used as practising material by the pupil for various surgical procedures such as incision making. The other kinds of stuff such as dummies and dead animals were also used. Different types of sutures and ligatures for clothes and bandaing on dummies were practiced. Since the actual surgery was to be performed on human bodies as such dead bodies on which dissections were to be performed and to be demonstrated were first kept covered with grass in the flowing water of the river. The muscles, internal organs and bones were studied after the skin has been peeled off. Susruta was well conscious of the fact that practical training is very much necessary for surgery. Therefore he stressed upon the importance of the same. His views are clearly brought out in Sanhita when he remarks :

"The physician who has learnt only bookish knowledge (bastras) but is unacquainted with the practical methods of treatment or the one who knows the practical details of the treatment but from self-confidence does not study the books is unfit to practice his profession. Such person deserves to be killed by the king".

MEDICAL BOTANY

The ayurvedic drugs and medicines are based upon herbs. A herbal garden for growing medicinal plants is desirable. This has also attracted the attention of Susruta who has given a detailed description of the medicinal plants and the soil best suited for their growth. Since the plant growing in a plot of land are also influenced with the property of soil on which it grow, the characterties of the ground best suited for the planting of medicinal herbs and trees are mentioned. He has given the requirement of the surface of the ground and has also mentioned that the ground chosen for plant should have not been a site of cremation or garbage dumps etc. The characteristics of the soil has been mentioned which according to Susruta should be glossary firm, steady, black, yellowish or red but free from sand, potash or other alkaline substances.

SUSRUTA AS MEDICAL METALLURGIST

This is one of the aspect of the versatile knowledge and genious of Susruta to have described the properties and uses of various metals and their compounds. In fact he has given the uses from the point of medicine and not from the consideration of metallurgy. In view of the fact that the uses of metals is important in ayurveda, Susruta has given the properties of such metals. Silver has been described to be laxative, destroying bile and wind but acidic taste. Zinc and lead has been stated as destroyer of worms in the body and of saline taste. Copper is corrosive, laxative in its potency, has sweet and astringent taste. Gold has many good properties from the medicine point of view. It is a tonic and balances the deranged humours of the body, it invigorates the eye sight and is cooling and antitoxic. It possesses a sweet and agreeable taste. The properties of pearls, corals, diamonds, sapphires, have also been mentioned from the point of view of the application in ayurvedic medicines.

9

Nagarjuna

A Scholar, A Scientist A Metallurgist

9

NAGARJUNA A SCHOLAR, A SCIENTIST A METALLURGIST

"Holy bank of river Ganges, near Patli putra, Hermitage made of bushes and wild grass; A lean and thin personality with no clothing around chest and head is busy in writing on Bhoj Patra in the dim light of twinkling earthen lamps in evening hours. The mighty king Kanishka accompanied by his scholar minister Ashaughosha are standing at the door step of the hermitage to have meeting with the lean man inside".

This is one of the true portrait of Nagarjuna who was reckoned as a top ranking philosopher, an eminent Buddhist scholar, a scientist, a technologist and a metallurgist par excellence.

The land of Vidharbha has the singular distinction to have given birth to Archarya Nagarjuna in 7-8 B.C. in a high and respected Brahmin family at Chhatisgarh. In those days Vidharbha was also known as south Kaushal and the same has been mentioned by Hiuen-Tsang, the famous Chinese traveller as the birth place of Nagarjuna. As per tradition prevailing in those days Nagarjuna made a thorough study of Vedas and vedangas at Patilputra which was a famous centre of learning, on the holy bank of River Ganges. Nagarjuna pursued the study under the pupilage of a competent Acharya since the age of 18 years. He made serious and concentrated study of Ayurveda and Buddhist philosophy. After having completed his study and with the blessing of his teachers. Nagarjun settled in a hermitage constructed at the bank of river at Gaya, which was a historical place. Many a philosophical works and treatises like Suhnllkha and Madhnic were written at this very hermitage High ranking scholars, experts of philosophy were all the time rallying around Nagarjun whose fame of scholarliness and knowledge was not only limited to Vidharbha and Gaya but to the entire country of India. History is silent to divulge as to who were the fortunate parents to have given birth to Nagarjun whose fame was touching the sky and there was no assembly or conference without the name of Nagarjun. The mightly king Kanishka was much influenced with Buddhism and accompanied with his Prime minister went to meet Nagarjun. The rays of the fame of Nagarjun found its way in the royal Darbar of King Satavahana who made Nagarjun as his envoy but even after being Rajguru, his living was not a grand palace but a hut or Ashram situated at the bank of river Krishna.

Three Nagarjunas **:** The study of various works and excerpts reveals that there have been more than one person with the name of Nagarjuna in different periods. Albureni has mentioned a personality with the name of Nagarjuna who has been a century before his arrival in India i.e. in 700 A.D. who was an expert with excellence in the science of chemistry. On the other hahd Hiuen-T. Sang-the Chinese traveller has also mentioned of a scholar with the name of Nagarjun who was capable to convert stone into gold. Again a famous work 'Rajtarangi' mentions that a great scholar with the name of Acharya Nagarjun has been 150 years after Lord Buddha. Thus, there had been three persons with the name of Nagarjun as under:

i) *Nagarjuna* of the period 150 years before (Lord Buddha mentioned in 'Rajtarnagini'.

ii) *Nagarjuna* as mentioned by Hiuen-T. Sang having been in first century A.D.

iii) *Nagarjuna* of 7th century A.D. as mentioned by Alberuni.

The meaningful details regarding first Nagarjun are not available in Rajtarangini except that he was Buddhist king. As regards the second Nagarjun, Hiuen-Tsang is clear to mention that he was Buddhist scholar and was capable to convert the stone into gold through the science of chemistry and he was very close friend as well as guru of king Shatvahan. In a very ancient book by Shatvahan's charioteer written on Bhojpatra, Nagarjuna has been mentioned as guru of king Shatvahan. It is mentioned that the Gupta rulers got the medical prescriptions given by Nagarjun engraved on pillars. The mention of Rahul Sanskritayana, the famous Buddhist monk also confirms that

Nagarjun was born in Vidharbh in South India and he was a disciple of Aashvghosha. As regards the Nagarjun which have been mentioned by Alberuni belonging to seventh century, nothing is known about his birth antencedants and its is possible that Alberuni without thorough investigations might have mentioned Naga arjun belonging to 7th century. However, it is difficult to say anything clearly and categorically.

Nagarjuna had written several books of high order and many of them are the treatise on philosophy, tantrism and spiritualism. The subject of some of the books is medical science. Works on metallurgy are also being attributed to Nagarjun. In nutshell, the works of Nagarjuna may be classified as under :

(i) Philosophy (ii) Tantrism

(iii) Medical science (iv) Metallurgy

The main books on Buddhist philosophy are nearly 20 and were translated by Kumarjiva in the year 405 A.D. On tantric science the main books include Tatav Parakash, Param Rahisya Sukabhi, Sambodhi, Samay Mudra etc.

Nagarjun has written an original and independent book on Opthamalogy which is known under the title 'Yen lung'. This book deals with the disease of eye treatment and diagnose on eye ailments. Yet one more book 'Adhishastra' the subject of which. Genetic science was also written by Nagarjun. One book on metallurgy, yet another book on Lohsastra (science of metals) is mentioned to have been written by Nagarjuna which, unfortunately is not available. Nagarjun has made a number of experiments on metals as well as medicines and it has been mentioned in 'Harash Charhita'. He presented two compendium of Rata Mala and Rashyan Gutika to the king Shatvahan which shows his science genious.

CONTRIBUTION MADE BY NAGARJUNA

Philosophy

Nagarjun was a distinguished philosopher and was contemporary to Asuaghosa, Aryadev and Kumaralabha who have been called four illuminating sun by Hiuen-Tsang. It was he who formulated the dotrine of the void (sunya or tathata) in his famous Madhyamika-sastra, which has won him a lasting place in world philosophy. In the same work he also distinguished between two truths, the conventional truth and the highest truth, without which it is not possible to understand either the void or Nirvana, which are matters not of intellectual grasp but of intuitive wisdom (Prajna). Other important works attributed to Nagarjuna are the Satasa harsrikaprajnaparamita, the Dasabhumi-vibhasa-sastra, and the Suhrillekha. I-Tsing speaks in high terms of the last work and observes that in his days it was widely read and memorized in India. Nagarjuna later became head of the University of Nalanda, and was succeeded there by his famous disciple Aryadeva, who was of Sinhalese origin. Aryadeva preached Buddhism for sometime in Prayaga, where he showed great courage in condemning the superstition of the multitude thronging to bathe in the river through his most famous work in Chatuh-Sataka. According to Winternitz, down to the present day, Nagarjuna's Madhyamika Sastra, together with Aryadeva's Chatuh-Sataka or Sata-Sastra, and the Dvadas-nikaya Sastra, form the groundwork of the faith of the sanron sect in Japan. All through the works of the famous trio, Asvaghosa, Nagarjuna and Aryadeva, the early patriarchs of the Mahayana, worship of the Buddha and absolute surrender (saranagati) for him are ardently expressed, along with the various metaphysical doctrines, as the key-notes of the new system of faith.

NAGARJUNA AS METALLURGIST AND ALCHEMIC:

The age of Nagarjuna was dominant with experiments on metals and mercury. He proved the uses of mercury by conducting hundreds of experiments in his laboratory and was successful to discover the wonderful power of mercury. As per Vag Bhatt, one of the mercury was of red colour which was most useful for alchemic purposes and was capable even to make the man almost immortal. The other kind of mercury was of light grey colour which was used by the people of Nag Desha against ageing. However, on account of invasions of foreigners, the sources of mining of red and grey mercury were closed down. Nagarjuna has written a number of scientific books one of which 'Yogsatak' has been published. One more work "Chitanand Patiasee" has been found in Tibet written on Bhoj Patra and it is not possible to give the complete account of the books Nagarjun wrote on the subject. Hiuen T-sang a famous Chinese traveller has mentioned Nagarjuna to be an expert in chemistry science and capable to convert stone into gold and this proves that Nagarjuna made unique discovery regarding various metals and mercury. These experiments relate not only to mercury but many other compounds of metals, sub-metals and non-metals.

The laboratory of Nagarjuna has been mentioned to be located at 'Sri Parvat' and there was a good collection of metal and submetals procured from far and wide. It has also been mentioned in certain works that many metals were imported from China, Greek, Tapti river etc. and various minerals were divided as : Rush Raj, Mha Rush Up Rush and Simple Rush. It has also been stated that Nagarjuna was aware as to which mercury could be converted into gold. A famous work 'Rush Ratanakar' has been written by Nagarjuna. It is, however not clear that this was the work of first Nagarjuna or second Nagarjuna or the last. Perusal of book shows the wonderful work done on the subject. It may be mentioned that there had been 27 experts and scientists of mercury and the detailed list of the names have been given in 'Ras Ratna Smuchy'. Out of this long list there are only four prominent names :

1. Nandi
2. Naga Arjuna
3. Munishwara
4. Som Deva

According to Veg Bhatt there have been no scholar of the science of Rasa more competent than the four names. In addition to these, there have been nearly 19 more scholars in the science of Rasa, however, Naga Arjuna surpasses all.

NAGARJUNA AS MEDICAL SCIENTIST

The unique contribution of Nagarjuna on the subject, is to write commentary on Susrut Sanhita and he made number of improvements therein. It may be mentioned that upto the period of Susrut Sanhita, though the various acharyas of Ayurveda were able to discover the usefulness of organic and in-organic elements and metals, however, Nagarjuna speltout the good uses of mercury as medicine and and as the unique power to cure various diseases more than all the organic and inorganic metals. On hundreds of diseases he proved the curing power of mercury in various forms. He has also been mentioned to have written an independent and original book on eye diseases dealing the subject of ophthalmology completely. Similarly on genetic science also he has written independent book.

10

Varamihra

Newton of Gupta Age

10

VARAMIHRA NEWTON OF GUPTA AGE

Varamihra was not only a great astronomer but was a scientist also. His work Punchsidhanta is considered to be the historical literature of Indian astronomical science. After the Vedic age there was a trend to study the horizon and the other contemporary developments resulting into exchange of views between Greek & India regarding astronomy and Varmihra is the astronomical scientist of this age. He was born towards the end of 5th century in Ujjain which was a part of Magadh empire (Madhya Bharat) in those days and was a son of Brahman Aditya Das. Varahmihra is the author of many works of astronomy and astrology and many of his books are still not available. All of his works could be divided into three parts:

i) Astronomy

ii) Astrology

iii) Agriculture.

Panchasiddhantika is the most outstanding work of Varahmihra which deals with 5 systems of astronomy as under :

i) Paitamaha

ii) Saurya

iii) Romaka

iv) Paulisa and

v) Vasistha Siddhantas

Out of which he assigns the first place to Saurya Sidshanta. As regards the Paitamaha Siddhantas though it attempts to lead to the prediction of solar eclipses but has been incapable of furnishing any rule to that end like other Indian astronomers.

Among five systems of astronomy described in Panchasiddhantika, the full text of treatise of only Saurya Siddhanta is available to us presently. The modern Saurya Siddhanta is very much the same in fundamental features as mentioned by Varahamihra. A cursory review of those chapters of the Panchasiddhantika treatise of the Saurya Siddhanta show at once that the treatise of the same known to Varamihra agreed with the modern Saurya Siddhanta. The methods of the two treatises are essentially the same and on the other hand sufficiently different from those of the other Siddhanta summarized by Varmihara to ensure the Saurya Siddhanta in its twofold form a distinct position of its own. But it must also be taken into account that the two treatises (the old we possess today) are different in many assential points and details. For example, the old Saurya Siddhanta assigned the mean diameters of the Sun and Moon the values 32'5" and 30'54" (Psi.IX.15-16) while according to the modern, the corresponding values are 32' 3.6" and 32' respectively.

There are other differences also between two Saurya Siddhanta in regard to the number of the years in a Maha Yuga, number of inter Calari months and omitted lunar days. Maha Yuga according to Varamihra will consist of twenty eight days less than that of modern Saurya Siddhanta days. Further there is a difference in respect to the mean revolution of the planets.

As regards Paitamaha Siddhanta, there is a small chapter devoted to the system in Panchasiddhantika and the five stanzas quoted in the chapter make clear the important substance of the siddhanta. The perusal of which shows that the siddhanta belongs to the same category as the Jyautisa Vedanga. and the Garga Samhita and it could be identified with them. According to which the Yuga contains sixty solar months, sixty two symbolical months etc.

According to the teaching of Pitamaha, five years constitute a Yuga of Sun and Moon. The adhimasas are brought about by thirty months and an omitted lunar day (avama) by sixty-two days.

Lessen the time of the Saka king by two, and divide by five; with the remaining years from the ahargana, which begins with the bright-half of Magha. The ahargana begins with the day, viz, from sunrise.

In the quinquennial luni-solar yuga of the Paitamaha Siddhanta, one adhimasa is comprised within each period of thirty solar months and one Avama, i.e. omitted lunar day within each of sixty two days.

According to this Stanza which directs us to deduct two from the number of elapsed Saka year, a new yuga began with 2 Saka elapsed.

If the ahargana is increased by its own sixty-first part, the result are the tithis. If it is multiplied by nine and divided by 122, the result is the namsatra of the Sun. Multiply the ahargana by 7, divide by 610 and deduct (the result from the ahargana), the result is the lunar maksatra, counting from Dhanistha.

REVOLVING OF EARTH

Varamihra regarded earth as an immovable sphere fixed at the centre of the universe around which the Sun, Moon and other planets revolved. A bird would not return to its nest as soon as it had flown away from it, had there been any motion in the earth. However, the modern astronomy has proved that the fact is otherwise. Regarding the position of the things on earth and its power he says that mountains, rivers, trees cities, men and angees all are around the globe of the earth and two cities are opposite to each other, it is difficult to say one is low in relation to the other. How can one say that one place of the earth is low as it is in every particular identical with another place of earth and one place could be as little flat as any other.

Varamihra has also written about astrology and Vrihat Jataka is the treatise on the subject which is still available but the subject of the work is limited to Horoscopy Astrology.

VARAMIHRA AS AN AGRONOMIST

This is yet another aspect of versatility of Varamihra. A section of his work Vrihat Samhita is devoted to the method for making the soil soft and suitable for sowing seeds or planting saplings. Varamihra described the method for better flowering and fruit formation as well as for the planting of saplings. and he suggested that the plant sapling should be first given bath in water. Various constellations in the sky are mentioned under whose influence the planting of the saplings leads to their better flourishing. The saplings whose branches and leaves are not yet developed are recommended to be planted in the months of January and February, those with just developed branches in the months of November and December and the ones with well developed branches in the months of June and July. Names are given of the trees which ought to be propagated by means of their cuttings. Grafting is described to be a better method which is done either by inserting the cutting of a plant on the roots or the stem of another plant. Cuttings and grafts are smeared over with cowdung. For transplanting, the plants are smeared over from root to top with clarified butter(ghee), Appropriate distance is left between two plants so that their roots do not intermingle because that leads to their ill functioning and the trees do not bear fruits. After planting, the trees are watered in the morning and evening in the summer, at the end of the day in winter and during the rainy season only when the earth is dry. Trees like Azadirachta (nim) are mentioned to be

conducive to the welfare of the house if planted in residential places.

DISEASES IN TREES

Varamihra has also suggested treatment to avoid diseases in trees resulting into non-development of the buds, dry branches and yellow leaves etc. As a general prophylactic measure against such exigencies, mud kneaded with ghee and vidanga is recommended to be applied to the roots and diluted milk poured around them. Varamihra says that a good growth of plants in a dry area indicates the presence of water under the soil.

It will thus be seen that Varamihra was a scientist who has dealt with various subjects like astronomy, astrology, agriculture, revolving of earth etc. He has mentioned various subjects on astronomy to know the divisions of time, ages, years, seasons, months, muhurtas, vipalas etc. as dealt by him in 5 siddhantas. While it is a fact that Varamihra's writing were influenced by Greek astronomy, his contribution is significant to the science of astrology though some of his views were either not correct as in many of his writings traditional views are reflected. In view of the religious and social environment prevailing in those days it will be uncharitable to blame him for his views and in the words of Alberuni "On the whole, his foot stands firmly on the basis of truth and he clearly calls out the truth".

11

Arya Bhata

The Founder of Algebra

11

ARYA BHATA THE FOUNDER OF ALGEBRA

"Aryabhata is the master who, after reaching the farthest shores and plumbing the inmost depths of the sea of ultimate knowlege of mathematics, kinematics and spherics, handed over the three sciences to the learned world".

Commentary on Aryabhatiya
by Bhaskara I

Aryabhatta was the first algebraist of ancient India and whatever he expounded was entirely his own contribution. After Vedanga-Jautisa where we have a glimpse of arithmeatic and algebra, supposed to be a work of 700 B.C., there has been a gap of nearly 700 years in Indian astronomy. Aryabhatta was a real astronomer and mathematician appeared in ancient

Indian horizon making a significant contribution in the new science known as algebra.

Ayrabhatta was born in 476 A.D. and is famous by his treatise Aryabhatiya which is a composition of 499 A.D. Though nothing is very clear about his birth place but the treatise which is a land mark in the field of science of algebra was composed in Kusumapura near Patna, Bihar.

TWO ARYABHATTAS

There have been two persons of same name as Aryabhatta and the great algebraist and scientist is Aryabhatt-I who wrote two treatise one at the age of 23 and another at an advance stage, only the later is available to us. What is more remarkable in the treatise is that the yuga supposed to begin from mid-night and the number of savana days in a Mahayuga exceeded by 300, though in the first treatise Yuga has been described to begin from the sunrise.

The treatise Aryabhattya is divided into 4 chapters called Padas. The first is called Gitika Pada (ii) Ganita Pada (iii) Kalakriya Pada (iv) Go a Pada. The first part containg 11 verses is the smallest chapter and only described the fruit of the study of these verses.

The most important chapter is the Ganita Pada which contains 33 verses, the subjects dealt with are squares, cubes, square root, cube root, area of a triangle and volume of a prism, area of a circle and volume of a sphere, area of a quadrilateral, circumference of a circle Rsine, determination of the Rsine of the zenith distance, the base of a right angled triangle and the upright of a right angled triangle, reversed sine, areas of circular figures, rule of three, reduction of fractions, inverse rule of three, evaluation of unknown values, and the theory of pulveriser.

The Kalakriya Pada containing only 23 verses deals with the units of time e.g. 12 months constitute one year, 30 days – one month, 60 nadi – one day, and 60 vinadis are equall to 24 minutes, the time taken by a normal man in having 6 breaths constitutes 24 seconds etc.

The Gqla Pada deals with the Sun's path, the ascending nodes of planets and the shadow of the Earth etc.

Contribution of Aryabhatta to the Science of Algebra, Astronomy and Geometry :

Foundation of Algebra laid – In the science of algebra Arya Bhatta gave the solution of many a problems of mathematics and also made new observation in geometry. The solution of the quadratic equation in algebra which was undetreminate first degree equation containing X^1 with value of X not obtainable in integral term was for the first time given by him, which is correct. The value of $\pi = 3.1416$ was obtained correct to the four places of decimal. The time of calculation of solar eclipse was the problem of astonomers which was solved by Arya Bhatta.

Quadratic Equation : This equation is applied to determine the interest in a problem quoted by Arya Bhatta. An amount of money loaned on unknown interest for six months and the interest is again loaned for a period and all together become Rs. 60. Arya Bhatta gives the solutions of the problem in a verse.

He also provided the solution of simultaneous type quardratic equation in a verse.

A notable achievement of Arya Bhatta was to give the concept of pulveriser and a process has been mentioned by him solving the same which is called Kutta and by this process he is perhaps the first in the history of mathematics in this regard and indeterminate equation of first degree could be solved by this process.

LINEAR EQUATIONS :

A linear equation in algebra in determining some unknown point in one of his verse is translated as under : The difference of the known "amount" relating to two persons should be divided by the difference of the coefficients of the unknown. The quotient will be the value of the unknown, if their possessions are equal.

All this show that a significant and outstanding contribution has been made by Arya Bhatta in the science of Algebra and infact he laid the foundation of Algebra in India.

GEOMETRY AND TRIGONOMETRY

The attainment of Arya Bhatta in Geometry and Trigonometry is marvelous where he has given various methods of solving following geometrical problems :

- Area of the triangle
- Area of the circle
- Circumference of the circle

- Volume of the sphere
- Value of π
- Method of Rsine

Aryabhatta gave a method of measuring the dimension of the shadow thrown by an object placed in part of light and this forming the basis of calculating the eclipse. Pythagaurian theorem was also described by him in one of his verses.

NOTATION OF NUMBERS

He devised a way of denoting of expressing the high number in measurement and used the stopped congonents to represent the nos. 1-25 when they preceded the vowel and high decimal powers of these numbers when they preceded other vowels as under :

a 1

i 100

u 100^2 or 10,000

r 100^3 or 1,000,000

lr 100^4 or 100,000,000

e 100^5 or 10,000,000,000

ai 100^6 or 1,000,000,000,000

o 100^7 or 100,000,000,000,000

au 100^8 or 10,000,000,000,000,000

The units, hundreds, ten thousands, one million etc., with odd placings are known as the vargasthana or the square positions, and tens, thousands, hundred thousands etc., with even number of digits are known as the average-sthana or the nonsquare positions. The India ancient system of digital counting in fact goes upto 10^{22} where in the count proceeds from 10^{16} das kharan to 10^{18} das padam, 10^{20} das neel and finally 10^{22} das padam.

ASTRONOMY

Arya Bhatta discarded the old views and made his own observations in the field of Astronomy. He threw to winds the belief that earth is static and anounced that the earth is a sphere rotating on its axis. Arya Bhatta developed the theory of epicycles to represent the motion of planet. He is the first to declare that lunar and solar eclipses are not caused by Rahu but by the shadow of earth on moon. He made it clear that moon is not self illuminated but it is dark and illuminated by Sun. He devised the method to predict the lunar and solar eclipses.

THE WORD 'SCIENCE' ORIGINATED FROM ARYA BHATTA

According to Amartya Sen-Noble laureate Arya Bhatta has named trigonometry "Jiya Ardha, from which the Arab word "Jeb" is derived. Later on Italian translated this to "Synous" from which the English word Science is derived.

(Reference Address by Prof. Amartya Sen - the Noble Prize winner at the Planery session of the Parvasi Bhartiya Divas celebration on 6th Jan. 2003)

In nutshell, Arya Bhatta is considered to be one of the greatest scientists of ancient India and algebraist par excellence. He is the first ancient mathematician to have made so significant contribution in the field of mathematics of algebra. Solution of indeterminate equation is one of the land marks to the credit of Arya Bhatta. Infact he is one of the most original scientists. He completely contradicted the orthodox view in the field of Astronomy to declare that the eclipses are not caused by Rahu but the shadow of moon on the earth and he was opposed bitterly by the contemporary as well as the mathematicians, astronomers of later times. The modern astronomy has vindicated his views.

ORIGINAL TEXT LOST

> ***"I have not been able to find any thing of the books of Arya Bhatta"***
>
> ***— Alberuni***

> ***"A long and diligence search failed to recover the aliphatic and other works of Arya Bhata"***
>
> ***— Cole Brook***

It is unfortunate that like many other ancient Indian scientists the original text of Arya Bhatta has been untraceable.

However, a text Arya Bhatiya was compiled later on and published in the year 1784 and it is on the basis of this book that the scientific genius of Arya Bhatta is known and his doctrine and treatise were made public.

12

Brahamgupta
A Great Mathematician

12

BRAHMA GUPTA
A GREAT MATHEMATICIAN

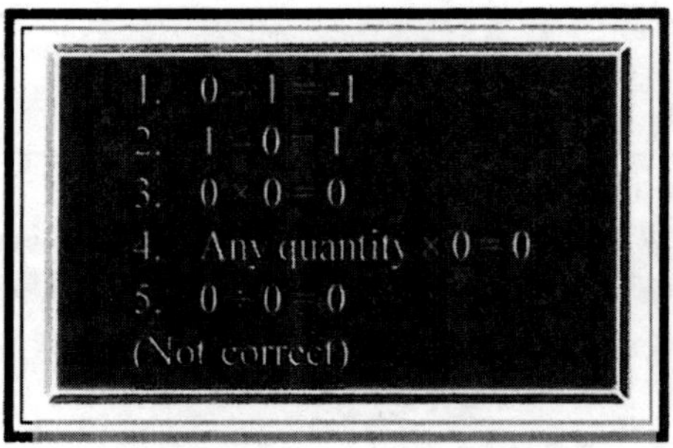

Brahma Gupta, according to Albruni – An Arab traveller who visited India around 1100 A.D, had been the most distinguished mathematician of ancient India. He was born in 598 A.D. in the town at Bhillamala near Multan, now in Pakistan. This was the period when the scientific activities were on the declining side on account of disturbed political situation in India.

There are two famous works attributed to Brahma Gupta-

(i) **Brahma's Sphuta Sidhanta** which he wrote when he was thirty years of age under the patronage of King Vyaghra Mukha of Chapa dynasty and is based upon his earlier work Pitamaha Sidhanta which had become outdated. What is remarkable is that in Sphutic Sidhanta, he has given his own independent views and latest knowledge in the subjects of Algebra, geometry, and astronomy and a comparison has been made with the views of other mathematicians as well as Hindu religious scriptures.

(ii) Karan Khanda Khadyaka is another work of Brahma Gupta which is believed to have been written in the year 665 A.D.

CONTRIBUTION OF BRAHMA GUPTA

Algebra – The most notable achievement of Brahma Gupta in the science of Algebra is the concept of zero - showing various aphorism with zero, like zero subtracted from a negative quantity will give negative, if subtracted from positive will give positive. Similarly zero multiplied by zero will give zero, if multiplied by any quantity will also give zero. But zero divided by zero according to him is also zero, which is wrong, as it will be an indeterminate quantity.

SOLUTION OF QUADRATIC EQUATION

Brahma Gupta had very high knowledge of algebra and gave simple rules for solving all types of simple quadratic equations. What is outstanding to his credit is giving the solution of indeterminate second-degree equation. The science of Algebra was taken a new height of excellence by him using the same for astronomical calculations.

GEOMETRY

In his book of Sphuta Sidhantha, Brahma Gupta gives the solution of various problems concerned to geometry. eg- solution of right angle triangle, properties of circle quadrilateral etc. He also gives the value of ratio of circumference of circle to its diameter. However, this value is less accurate than that of Arya Bhatta.

CONTRIBUTION IN THE SCIENCE OF ASTRONOMY

In his work of Sphuta Sidhantha, Brahma Gupta gives the methods of calculation of motions of various planets, Moon and Sun eclipses and system of Astronomy. He reiterated the views of Arya Bhatta that the Earth is round in shape. According to him, stars rise and set in different places at different times on account of the fact that Earth was round. A more significant observation of Brahma Gupta was gravitational force of Earth. It was he who for the first time hinted that Earth has attractive force and he attributed it to the nature of Earth to keep things. However he was not correct to say that Earth is stationary and does not rotate, opined by Arya Bhatta. His observation regarding the cause of eclipses was also not correct. He criticized the view of Arya Bhatta that the eclipses are on account of shadow of moon on Earth and not by Rahu. He has been described as the most distinguished astronomer of his times by Albruni. It appears that he has perhaps bowed down to the prevailing orthodox views described in Puranas regarding eclipses and non-rotation of Earth. Brahma Gupta was under the patronage of the king who may be holding the same views as such speaking out his correct views would have been in bad taste and would not have been likable to the King and the then prevailing Brahmin religion which believed in the orthodox astronomical views.

In nut shell the outstanding achievements of Brahma Gupta were- concept of zero, solution of indeterminate second-degree equation in algebra and taking the science of Algebra to new heights by using the same in astronomical calculations.

13

Bhaskara
The Great Algebraist and Astronomer

13

BHASKARA - THE GREAT ALGEBRAIST AND ASTRONOMER

In Medieval India when Hindu sciences were showing the sign of decadence, the horizon of mathematics was illuminated by a shining star - Bhaskara, the great mathematician. There have been two personalities in the same name and both being mathematician as under :

1. Bhaskara - I 470 A.D.
2. Bhaskara - II 1142 A.D.

However, it is Bhaskara II who finds a high place amongst astronomers and mathematicians of India and made a valuable contribution in these fields, which inspired many of the astronomers particularly in the science of Algebra.

BIRTH AND AGE OF BHASKARA

'Mathematician son of Mathematician father' is the appropriate description of Bhaskara's family as his father Mahesvara who was his teacher also, was a mathematician. Bhaskara's son was astronomer as well as mathematician and got royal patronage on account of his eminence in mathematics and astronomy. Bhaskara was born at Vijjadavida in Shahya dry Hills which is a part of modern Maharashtra State, in the year 1114 A.D. The family tree of Bhaskara has been given in some of the text as under :

Trivikrama - Bhaskara Bhatta - Govinda - Prabhakara - Manoratha - Mahesvara - Bhaskara - Laksmidhara - Gangadeva.

WORK OF BHASKARA

Bhaskara is the celebrated author of the following treatises which are highly popular even now :

1. The Siddhantasiromani
2. The Marana - Kutuhala

Siddhantasiromani is the most famous one and has four parts and Leelawati is the first, known as Patiganita and contains 278 verses. Though the work is independent one, however, not the original as writing of the earliest scholars Arya Bhatta, Brahama Gupta, Shridhara, form the essential base of the work. The Patiganita deals with the various units of weight & measure and 20 Arithmatic operations i.e. addition, substraction, multiplication, division square, square root, cube and cube root, eight operations of substraction etc. What is more important is the solution of indeterminate equation beside second degree equations etc.

SIDDHANTA-SHIROMANI PART-II

This is known as Biz-gantia and comprises of 230 verses and deals with the concept and negative and positive numerals, negative & positive unknown quantities, rules of subtraction and addition, multiplication & division. The interesting findings are as under :

The square of a positive or a negative quantity is positive, but the square root of a positive quantity could be either positive or negative. The square root of a negative quantity cannot be derived.

UNKNOWN QUANTITY

Bhaskara in his Bijj-Ganita says that unknown quantity can be added or substracted from the one of the same kind not from the different one. In mathematical terms it means that 2a could be added to or substracted from 6a or 8a or 9a but not from 5b or 5c etc. Similarly $5a^3$ could be added or substracted to $3a^3$, $5a^3$, $4a^3$ and so on. He also mentioned as to how unknown quantity could be represented and he suggested that the name of colours like kalka, Pataka, Vahitaka should be used for the purpose. Bhaskara also made considerable progress in every abbreviated notation and instead of using entire word he has stipulated a method of writing device to donate a division of a quantity by an another quantity.

BHASKARA'S ASTRONOMY

The subject of astronomy has been dealt in his treastise of Ganita Adhyaya and Gola Adhyaya of Siddhanta Shiromani, Bhaskara attributed the motion of the planets to weather which he derived from atmospheric currents. He developed a theory to analyse the motion of Sun. Bhaskara's astronomy is more or less based upon Surya Siddhanta.

POPULARITY OF BHASKARA'S TREATISES

The treatises of Bhaskara are highly popular as number of commentaries were written on them. His work Leelawati was translated under the title "Algebra with Arithmatic of Braham Gupta and Bhaskara in the year 1817 by H.T. Colebrood. An English version of Leelawati was done by J. Tylore in the year 1816. Similarly Bhaskara's Bij-Ganita was also translated in London in the year 1817.

Akbar the great Mugal got the Leelawati and Bijja-Ganita translated into Persian in the year 1578 and 1634 A.D. respectively. In nutshell Bhaskara's contribution to arithmatic and algebra is significant and will also be remembered.

CONCEPTION OF ZERO

As regards Bhaskara, the statement of zero more or less appears to be based upon Brahama Gupta. He says that zero added or subtracted from a quantity does not change a number. Also the product will be zero if any quantity is multiplied by zero or zero multiplied by any quantity. Similarly zero divided by any quantity could furnish zero. He however, corrected the conception of Brahama Gupta when he says that any quantity divided by zero would be determinate infinite. To an infinite quantity if any thing is added or substracted, it will remain infinite without causing any material difference.

14

Bibliography

BIBLIOGRAPHY

(In addition to that given in references with every chapter)

Alberuni's Indica (1031A.D.)

Aryabhatiya (1930)

Trans. with notes by Walter Eugene Clark.

Atharvaveda-Samhita (1905)

English Trans. by W.D. Whitney.

Basham A.L. (1954)

The Wonder that was India. Sidgwick and Jackson, London.

Beal Samuel (1958)

Travels of Hiuen-Tsang Vol. I.

Bentley John (1825)

Historical View of Hindu Astronomy.

Burgess E. (1935)

English translation of the Surya-siddhanta.

Caraka Samhita (1949)

English version.

Datta B.B. (1932)

The Science of the Sulbas, Univ. of Calcutta.

Jaggi O.P.

Scientists of Ancient India.

Karambelkar V.W. (1961)

The Atharva Veda and the Ayurveda. Publisher Ku. Usha Karambelkar Tulsi bag Rd., Nagpur.

Kaye G.R. (1924)

Hindu Astronomy.

Keith A.B. (1921)

Indian Logic and Atomism.

Kutumbiah P. (1962)

Ancient Indian Medicine, Orient Longman's Ltd., Madras.

Majumdar R.C. (1952 to 1965)

The History and Culture of the Indian People.

Max Muller (1882)

Heritage of India.

Mishra Umesh (1936)

Conception of Matter. Allahabad.

Mookerji R.K. (1957)

Indian Shipping. 2nd Ed. Longmans, Madras.

Mukhopadhayaya G.N. (1923 to 1926)

History of Indian Medicine 2 vols. Univ. of Calcutta.

Ravi Varma (1940)

Ayurveda and Technical Sciences.

Satya Prakash (1965)

Founders of Sciences in Ancient India. The Research Instt. of Ancient Scientific Studies. New Delhi.

Seal B.N. (1958)

The Positive Sciences of Ancient Hindus.

Susruta Samhita (1907-8)

Trans. into English by Kaviraj Kunja Lal Bhishagaratna, Calcutta.

Zimmer H. (1948)

Hindu Medicine. The Johns Hopkins Press, Baltimore.